Linux Shell Scripting Essentials

Learn shell scripting to solve complex shell-related
problems and efficiently automate your day-to-day tasks

Sinny Kumari

BIRMINGHAM - MUMBAI

Linux Shell Scripting Essentials

First published: November 2015

Production reference: 1161115

Published by Packt Publishing Ltd.
Livery Place
35 Livery Street
Birmingham B3 2PB, UK.

ISBN 978-1-78528-444-1

www.packtpub.com

Credits

Author
Sinny Kumari

Reviewers
Grigor Aslanyan

Mohamed Fawzy

John Kennedy

Commissioning Editor
Pramila Balan

Acquisition Editor
Sonali Vernekar

Content Development Editor
Shali Deeraj

Technical Editors
Naveenkumar Jain

Mitali Somaiya

Copy Editor
Trishya Hajare

Project Coordinator
Sanchita Mandal

Proofreader
Safis Editing

Indexer
Priya Subramani

Production Coordinator
Nitesh Thakur

Cover Work
Nitesh Thakur

About the Author

Sinny Kumari has been a GNU/Linux user since the beginning of her college days. Her passion is to contribute to free software that benefits millions of people. She is a KDE contributor, KDE e.V. member, Fedora packager, and a Google Summer of Code mentor.

To keep up her passion in open source, she has been working as a software engineer at Red Hat after completing her bachelor's degree in computer science in 2012. As part of her work, she contributes to the Libabigail project that helps with ABI analysis on ELF binaries. She also loves going to technical conferences and sharing her experiences by giving talks. Her blogs about almost all of these activities can be found at `http://sinny.io/`.

I want to thank my parents who have always supported, encouraged, and provided me with the best education. I would also like to thank my friends and family who were always around me to cheer me up. Special thanks to my friend, Shantanu Tushar, who clarified a few doubts I came across while writing this book. I would also like to thank the reviewers of this book and the entire PacktPub team.

About the Reviewers

Grigor Aslanyan is a theoretical cosmologist with a strong focus on computational methods for data analysis. He has a PhD in physics from the University of California, San Diego, and is currently a postdoctoral research fellow at the University of Auckland in New Zealand.

Grigor was born and raised in Armenia. He obtained both bachelor's and master's degrees in physics and computer science at Yerevan State University, before moving to California for his PhD studies. He has also worked as a software engineer for three years at Ponté Solutions (a company later acquired by Mentor Graphics).

Grigor's research focuses on studying the theory of the very early universe by using experimental data from cosmic microwave background radiation and galaxy surveys. His research requires the development and implementation of complex numerical tools used to analyze the data on large computational clusters, with the ultimate goal of learning about the theory of the early universe. Grigor's current research is focused on applying advanced data science and machine learning techniques to improve data analysis methods in cosmology, making it possible to analyze the large amounts of data expected from the current and future generation experiments.

Grigor has implemented the publicly available numerical library Cosmo++ that includes general mathematical and statistical tools for data analysis as well as cosmology-specific packages. The library is written in C++ and is publicly available at http://cosmopp.com.

I would like to thank the University of Auckland and my supervisor Richard Easther for supporting my work on this book.

Mohamed Fawzy is an open source geek who adores working with servers. He has been working with Linux since 2013 — working and delivering training in Linux system engineering. He has many contributions in open source communities, especially in Egypt where he is a Fedora project contributor and ambassador. He currently lives in Egypt and studies in Mansoura University.

I would like to express my deepest appreciation to all those who have provided me the opportunity to achieve my life goals.

I want to express my warm thanks to my family, especially my father who always supports me. I would like to thank my friends, Mohamed Desoky and Yomna Hafez who are engineers, and also my team, CatReloaded, and its core members, especially Amira, for my graduation project, Fedora. I would also like to thank all the contributors who work as friends, Levex, Zoltan, and others, for their support and guidance in my life.

Special gratitude I give to our project manager, Sanchita Mandal, who coordinated the project well, the writer who did her best to write this book, and Packt Publishing.

Thanks to you all for being in my life.

John Kennedy has worked with UNIX and Linux since 1998. He has been shell scripting since 2001. His preferred language is BASH, although he has dabbled in Python.

He has been reviewing and tech-editing books in his spare time since 2001 and has about 20 books under his belt. He believes the best part of reviewing is that he learns something from every book he works on.

John was born in the US and grew up in Northern Virginia. He spent some time in the US Air Force and has lived in Germany and the United Kingdom. He is married to Michele and has two children, Denise and Kieran. He currently lives in Northern Virginia.

I would like to thank my family including my nephews, Aiden and Mason, and my niece, Harriet, for supporting all the silly things I do and for giving me the time to work on this.

I would also like to thank Sanchita Mandal who possesses great patience and flexibility and was very supportive. Also, my thank go to the author, Sinny Kumari who made this book easy to review and educational to read. Everyone at Packt also deserves recognition for all the titles and hard work that goes into producing them.

www.PacktPub.com

Support files, eBooks, discount offers, and more

For support files and downloads related to your book, please visit
www.PacktPub.com.

Did you know that Packt offers eBook versions of every book published, with PDF
and ePub files available? You can upgrade to the eBook version at www.PacktPub.
com and as a print book customer, you are entitled to a discount on the eBook copy.
Get in touch with us at service@packtpub.com for more details.

At www.PacktPub.com, you can also read a collection of free technical articles,
sign up for a range of free newsletters and receive exclusive discounts and offers
on Packt books and eBooks.

https://www2.packtpub.com/books/subscription/packtlib

Do you need instant solutions to your IT questions? PacktLib is Packt's online digital
book library. Here, you can search, access, and read Packt's entire library of books.

Why subscribe?

- Fully searchable across every book published by Packt
- Copy and paste, print, and bookmark content
- On demand and accessible via a web browser

Free access for Packt account holders

If you have an account with Packt at www.PacktPub.com, you can use this to access
PacktLib today and view 9 entirely free books. Simply use your login credentials for
immediate access.

Table of Contents

Preface

The shell on a GNU/Linux system is arguably the most powerful tool for any user. In general terms, the shell serves as an interface between the system's user and the operating system kernel. We use the shell to run commands in order to perform tasks and frequently save the output to files. While these simple use-case are easy to achieve by just using some commands on the shell, sometimes the task at hand is more complex than that.

Enter shell scripting, the magical tool that allows you to write step-by-step instructions to the shell on how to perform a complex task. However, just learning the syntax to write scripts is not enough unless you know the commands at your disposal. Only then would scripts be reusable, efficient, and easy to use. When one has mastered the commands available on a GNU/Linux system, what follows is a frenzy to automate daily tasks—be it finding documents or cleaning up old movies that have long been watched. Whether you're an expert with other scripting languages or you're doing this for the first time, this book will show you how to do magic with shell scripts!

What this book covers

Chapter 1, *The Beginning of the Scripting Journey*, tells you about the importance of writing shell scripts along with a simple Hello World shell script program. It also covers the basic and essential shell script topics such as defining a variable, built-in variables, and operators. It also contains a detailed explanation of shell expansion that occurs with characters such as ~, *, ?, [], and {}.

Chapter 2, *Getting Hands-on with I/O, Redirection Pipes, and Filters*, talks about the standard input, output, and error streams for a command and shell script. It also has instructions on how to redirect them to other streams. One of the most powerful concepts, namely regular expressions, is also covered. It serves as instructions to commands such as `grep`, `sed`, `uniq`, and `tail` for filtering useful data from input data.

Chapter 3, Effective Script Writing, provides an insight into structuring shell scripts to organize tasks. After talking about script exit codes, it talks about basic programming constructs such as conditionals and loops. It then goes on to discuss the organization of code into functions and aliases. Finally, it wraps up with details on how `xargs`, `pushd`, and `popd` works.

Chapter 4, Modularizing and Debugging, talks about making shell scripts modular by using common code that can be sourced. It also covers the details of command line arguments to scripts and how one can debug their scripts when they malfunction. This chapter also contains information on how the user can implement custom command completion.

Chapter 5, Customizing the Environment, moves on to talk about the shell environment—what it contains, its significance, and finally how to modify it. It also takes the reader through the different initialization files that bash uses at startup. Finally, we talk about how to check command history and manage running tasks.

Chapter 6, Working with Files, talks about files, which are the entities that most of any UNIX system is composed of. It covers the basic philosophy of "everything is a file" and takes the reader through basic file operations, comparing files, finding them, and creating links. This chapter then explains what special files and temporary files are, and the details involved in file permissions.

Chapter 7, Welcome to the Processes, talks about executable files that come alive—and become processes. From listing and monitoring running processes, it goes on to talk about how to exploit process substitution. Next, it covers process scheduling priorities, signals, traps, and how processes can communicate with each other.

Chapter 8, Scheduling Tasks and Embedding Languages in Scripts, discusses scheduling tasks at appropriate times by using the system Cron. Next, it covers systems that are responsible for orchestrating startup tasks in most modern Linux systems. Finally, this chapter contains instructions on how to embed scripts from other scripting languages into a shell script.

What you need for this book

The reader doesn't require any previous knowledge to understand this book, though some familiarity with Linux will help. On the software side, a recent enough Linux distribution with bash 4 should be able to try out all examples in this book.

Who this book is for

This book is aimed at administrators and those who have the basic knowledge of shell scripting and want to learn how to get the most out of writing shell scripts.

Conventions

In this book, you will find a number of text styles that distinguish between different kinds of information. Here are some examples of these styles and an explanation of their meaning.

Code words in text, database table names, folder names, filenames, file extensions, pathnames, dummy URLs, user input, and Twitter handles are shown as follows: "We can also use the `printf` command in shell programming for printing."

A block of code is set as follows:

```
$ name=foo
$ foo="Welcome to foo world"
$ echo $name
foo
$ new_name='$'$name     #new_name just stores string value $foo
$ echo $new_name
$foo
$ eval new_name='$'$name  # eval processes $foo string into variable
and  prints                # foo variable value
Welcome to foo world
```

Any command-line input or output is written as follows:

```
$ ps -p $$
```

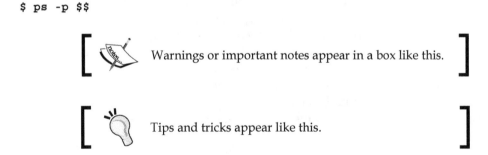

> Warnings or important notes appear in a box like this.

> Tips and tricks appear like this.

Reader feedback

Feedback from our readers is always welcome. Let us know what you think about this book—what you liked or disliked. Reader feedback is important for us as it helps us develop titles that you will really get the most out of.

To send us general feedback, simply e-mail feedback@packtpub.com, and mention the book's title in the subject of your message.

If there is a topic that you have expertise in and you are interested in either writing or contributing to a book, see our author guide at www.packtpub.com/authors.

Customer support

Now that you are the proud owner of a Packt book, we have a number of things to help you to get the most from your purchase.

Downloading the example code

You can download the example code files from your account at http://www.packtpub.com for all the Packt Publishing books you have purchased. If you purchased this book elsewhere, you can visit http://www.packtpub.com/support and register to have the files e-mailed directly to you.

Errata

Although we have taken every care to ensure the accuracy of our content, mistakes do happen. If you find a mistake in one of our books—maybe a mistake in the text or the code—we would be grateful if you could report this to us. By doing so, you can save other readers from frustration and help us improve subsequent versions of this book. If you find any errata, please report them by visiting http://www.packtpub.com/submit-errata, selecting your book, clicking on the **Errata Submission Form** link, and entering the details of your errata. Once your errata are verified, your submission will be accepted and the errata will be uploaded to our website or added to any list of existing errata under the Errata section of that title.

To view the previously submitted errata, go to https://www.packtpub.com/books/content/support and enter the name of the book in the search field. The required information will appear under the **Errata** section.

Piracy

Piracy of copyrighted material on the Internet is an ongoing problem across all media. At Packt, we take the protection of our copyright and licenses very seriously. If you come across any illegal copies of our works in any form on the Internet, please provide us with the location address or website name immediately so that we can pursue a remedy.

Please contact us at `copyright@packtpub.com` with a link to the suspected pirated material.

We appreciate your help in protecting our authors and our ability to bring you valuable content.

Questions

If you have a problem with any aspect of this book, you can contact us at `questions@packtpub.com`, and we will do our best to address the problem.

1
The Beginning of the Scripting Journey

Unix, Unix-like, or Linux-based OS provide a lot of powerful features to work upon. Among them, the most powerful and important feature is executing a wide range of commands to perform a task quickly and easily; for example, `ls`, `cat`, `sort`, `grep`, and so on. We will come to know about a subset of commands and usages throughout this book. In order to run a command, we need an interface that is widely known as **shell**.

Shell is a program that acts as an interface between the users (we) and the OS kernel (Linux, Unix, and so on). Understanding in terms of Windows OS, shell serves a similar purpose DOS does. Different shells are available for Unix, Unix-like, or Linux OS. Some of the popular shells are Bourne shell (sh), C shell (csh), Korn shell (ksh), Bourne Again shell (bash), and Z shell (zsh).

In this book, we will be using Linux OS and Bourne Again shell, popularly known by its acronym `bash`. Linux-based systems generally have `bash` already installed. In case `bash` is not installed, try installing the bash package from your distribution's package manager. In order to know which shell currently your Linux console is using, run the following command in terminal:

```
$ ps -p $$
```

The output is as follows:

```
  PID TTY          TIME CMD
12578 pts/4    00:00:00 bash
```

In the preceding ouput, we see that the CMD column has value `bash`. This means, we are currently using `bash` shell in our current console.

If your console is not using the bash shell, then you can run the following command:

```
$ bash
```

Also, your shell will be bash now. To make bash as a default login shell, run the following command:

```
$ chsh -s /bin/bash
```

The output obtained is as follows:

```
Changing shell for user.
Password:******
Shell changed.
```

We are now set with bash shell and ready to learn shell scripting in detail. Shell scripts are nothing but plain text files with a series of commands that are run by bash in a specified order. Writing shell scripts is very useful when you have to perform a series of tasks by running various commands, as bash will read each line from a script file and run it without any need of user intervention. The general file extension used for shell scripts are .sh, .bash, .zsh, .ksh, and so on. Rather than using a file extension for shell scripts, it's preferred to keep a filename without extension and let an interpreter identify the type by looking into shebang (#!). Shebang is used in scripts to indicate an interpreter for execution. It is written in the first line of a script file, for example:

```
#! /bin/bash
```

It means use the bash shell to execute a given script. To run a shell script, make sure it has execute permission. To provide execute permission to an owner of a file, run the following command:

```
$ chmod u+x foo
```

Here, foo is the shell script file. After running this command, foo will have execute permission for the owner of the file.

Now, we are ready to proceed further on learning shell scripting concepts in detail. Each topic and subtopic covered in the chapters with examples will lead us progressively towards a good shell script programmer.

In this chapter, we will talk broadly about the following topics:

- Hello World in shell
- Define variables of choice
- Builtin shell variables

- Operators
- Shell expansions
- Construct commands using eval
- Make bash behave using set

Hello World in shell

Whenever we learn a new programming language, we first learn how to write the Hello World program in it. It is the best way to know and interact with a new language. This also helps in confirming that the basic environment for a program in a given language has been set up and you are good to dive deep inside this language.

Interacting with shell

We can print the output of commands in console in an interactive way. Console is also known as a standard input and output stream. To print anything in a bash console, use the echo command followed by what is to be printed:

```
$ echo Hello World
Hello World
```

Alternatively, put the text to be printed in double quotes:

```
$  echo "Hello World"
Hello World
```

You can also put the text to be printed in single quotes:

```
$ echo 'Hello World'
Hello World
```

We can also use the printf command in shell programming for printing. The printf command also supports formatted printing, similar to what we have in C programming language— the printf( ) function:

```
$ printf "Hello World"
Hello World$
```

Here, after the output, we see the command prompt ($) because printf doesn't add a default newline after execution while echo does. So, we have to explicitly add the newline (\n) in the printf statement to add a newline:

```
$ printf "Hello World\n"
Hello World
```

Similar to the C `printf ( )`, we can specify formatted printing in `bash`. The syntax of `bash` `printf` is as follows:

```
printf FORMAT [ARGUMENTS]
```

FORMAT is a string that describes the format specifications and is specified within double quotes. ARGUMENTS can be the value or a variable corresponding to format specification. Format specification consists of the percentage (%) sign followed by format specifier. Format specifiers are explained in the following table:

Format specification	Description
%u	This prints an unsigned integer value
%i or %d	This prints an associated argument as a signed number
%f	This prints an associated argument as a floating point number
%o	This prints an unsigned octal value
%s	This prints a string value
%X	This prints an unsigned hexadecimal value (0 to 9 and A to F)
%x	This prints an unsigned hexadecimal value (0 to 9 and a to f)

The following examples demonstrate how to use format specification for printing different data type format in shell:

```
$ printf "%d mul %f = %f\n" 6 6.0 36.0
6 mul 6.000000 = 36.000000
$ printf "%s Scripting\n" Shell
Shell Scripting
```

We can also optionally specify a modifier in format specification to align an output to provide better formatting to the output. Format modifiers are placed between % and the format specifier character. The following table explains format modifiers:

Format Modifiers	Description
N	This is any number that specifies a minimum field width.
.	This is used together with field width. The field doesn't expand when the text is longer.
-	This is the left-bound text printing in the field.
0	This is used to fill padding with zeros (0) instead of whitespaces. By default, padding is done with whitespaces.

The following example demonstrates how to use format modifiers to improve printing formatting:

```
$ printf "%d mul %.2f = %.2f\n" 6 6.0 36.0
6 mul 6.00 = 36.00
```

Let's make it scripted

Interactive printing is good if we have to print one or two lines, but for a lot of printing, it's good and preferred to write a script file. A script file will contain all the instructions and we can run a script file to perform the needed task.

Now, we are going to create a bash script file that makes use of the echo and printf commands and print messages:

```
#!/bin/bash
#Filename: print.sh
#Description: print and echo

echo "Basic mathematics"
printf "%-7d %-7s %-7.2f =\t%-7.2f\n" 23 plus 5.5 28.5
printf "%-7.2f %-7s %-7d =\t%-7.2f\n" 50.50 minus 20 30.50
printf "%-7d %-7s %-7d =\t%-7d\n" 10 mul 5 50
printf "%-7d %-7s %-7d =\t%-7.2f\n" 27 div 4 6.75
```

The first line in bash script represents the path of the interpreter used. The second line is a comment line telling the filename of a script file. In shell script, we use # to add a comment. Furthermore, the echo command will print strings written within double quotes. For the rest, we have used printf to print formatted output.

To run this script, we will first provide execute permission to a user/owner of this script:

```
$ chmod u+x print.sh
```

Then, run the script file in console as follows:

```
$ ./print.sh
```

The result after running this script will look as follows:

```
Basic mathematics
23      plus    5.50    =       28.50
50.50   minus   20      =       30.50
10      mul     5       =       50
27      div     4       =       6.75
```

Define variables of choice

Now we know how to write a simple hello world shell script. Next, we will be getting familiar with variables in shell and how to define and use variables in shell.

Nomenclature

A variable name can be a combination of alphanumeric and underscore. Also, the name of the variable can't start with a number. The variable names in shell script are case-sensitive. Special characters, such as *, -, +, ~, ., ^, and so on, are not used in variable names because they have a special meaning in shell. The following table illustrates the correct and incorrect ways of naming a variable:

Correct variable names	Incorrect variable names
variable	2_variable
variable1	2variable
variable_2	variable$
_variable3	variable*^

Assigning a value

We can assign a value to a variable by using an assignment (=) operator and followed by a value. While assigning a variable value, there shouldn't be any space before and after the assignment operator. Also, a variable can't be declared alone; it has to be followed by its initial value assignment:

```
$ book="Linux Shell Scripting"  # Stores string value
$ book = "Linux Shell Scripting"  # Wrong, spaces around = operator
$ total_chapters=8    # Stores integer value
$ number_of_pages=210    # Stores integer value
$ average_pages_per_chapter=26.25    # Stores float value
```

So, it's quite easy to declare and assign a value to a variable in shell script. You don't have to worry about the data type of a variable on the left-hand side. Whatever value you provide on the right-hand side, the variable stores that value.

Downloading the example code

You can download the example code files from your account at http://www.packtpub.com for all the Packt Publishing books you have purchased. If you purchased this book elsewhere, you can visit http://www.packtpub.com/support and register to have the files e-mailed directly to you.

Accessing a value

To access a variable value, use a dollar sign ($) operator followed by a variable name:

```
#!/bin/bash
#Filename: variables.sh
#Description: Basic variable definition and accessing them

book="Linux Shell Scripting"
total_chapters=8
number_of_pages=210
average_pages_per_chapter=26.25

echo "Book name - $book"
echo "Number of Chapters - $total_chapters"
printf "Total number of pages in book - $number_of_pages\n"
printf "Average pages in each chapter - %-.2f\n" $average_pages_per_
chapter
```

The result of this script will look as follows:

```
Book name - Linux Shell Scripting
Number of Chapters - 8
Total number of pages in book - 210
Average pages in each chapter - 26.25
```

We can remove the value of a variable using the unset keyword in bash. Using unset to a variable deletes and resets it to null:

```
#!/bin/bash
#Filename: unset.sh
#Description: removing value of a variable

fruit="Apple"
quantity=6
echo "Fruit = $fruit , Quantity = $quantity"
unset fruit
echo "Fruit = $fruit , Quantity = $quantity"
```

The result after running this script will look as follows:

```
Fruit = Apple , Quantity = 6
Fruit =  , Quantity = 6
```

It's clear that we used unset on a fruit variable, so when we try to access a variable fruit after unsetting it in line no. 8, it prints nothing. The quantity variable still retains its value because we haven't used unset on it.

Constant variables

We can also create the constant variable in bash whose value can't be changed. The readonly keyword is used to declare a constant variable. We can also use declare -r followed by a variable name to make it constant:

```
#!/bin/bash
#Filename: constant.sh
#Description: constant variables in shell


readonly text="Welcome to Linux Shell Scripting"
echo $text
declare -r number=27
echo $number
text="Welcome"
```

The result after running this script will look as follows:

```
Welcome to Linux Shell Scripting
27
constant.sh: line 9: text: readonly variable
```

From the error message, it's clear that we can't change the value of a constant variable, and also we can't unset the value of the constant variable.

Reading variables from a user input

We can ask the user to provide input using the read shell built in command. The number of inputs to be given by a user is equivalent to the number of arguments provided to read. The value inserted by a user is stored in respective parameters passed to read. All parameters act as variables in which the corresponding user input value is stored.

The syntax of read is as follows:

```
read [options] var1 var2   … varN
```

If no variable in an argument is specified, the input value by a user will be stored in the inbuilt variable REPLY and can be accessed further using $REPLY.

We can read a user input in its input variable as follows:

```
$ read
    Hello World
$ echo $REPLY
    Hello World
```

We can read a value from user input as follows:

```
$ read text
    Hello
$ echo $text
    Hello
```

We can read multiple values from user input as follows:

```
$ read name usn marks
    Foo 345 78
$ echo $name $usn $marks
    Foo 345 78
```

We can read only the n characters and don't wait for the user to input a complete line as follows:

```
$ read -n 5      # option -n number takes only 5 characters from user
input
    Hello$
$ echo $REPLY
    Hello
```

We can prompt the user a message before reading user input as follows:

```
$ read -p "What is your name?"     # -p allows to prompt user a message
    What is your name?Foo
$   echo $REPLY
    Foo
```

Hiding an input character when reading in console:

```
$   read -s -p "Enter your secret key:"  # -s doesn't echo input in
console
Enter your secret key:$     #Pressing enter key brings command prompt $
echo $REPLY
foo
```

The following example shows the `read` command's usage:

```
#!/bin/bash
#Filename: read.sh
#Description: Find a file in a path entered by user

read -p "Enter filename to be searched:"
filename=$REPLY
read -p "Enter path for search:" path
echo "File $filename search matches to"
find $path -name $filename
```

The following is the result of running the `read.sh` script in `bash`:

```
Enter filename to be searched:read
Enter path for search:/usr/bin
File read search matches to
/usr/bin/read
```

Here, the `find` command has been used to search for the filename in the specified path. The detailed discussion of the command `find` will be done in *Chapter 6, Working with Files*.

Builtin shell variables

Builtin shell variables are predefined and are global variables that we can use in our script at any point of time. These are reserved shell variables and some of them may have a default value assigned by `bash`. Some variables' value will depend upon your current shell environment setup. The different type of shell may have a few specific reserved variables to it. All builtin shell variables' name will be in uppercase.

A few reserved shell variables available in `bash` shell are as follows:

Shell variables available in bash	Description
BASH	This is the absolute path of the current bash being invoked
BASH_VERSION	This is the version number of bash
BASHPID	This is the process ID of the current bash process
EUID	This is the effective user ID of the current user, which is assigned during startup

Shell variables available in bash	Description
HOME	This is the current user's home directory
HOSTNAME	This is the name of the current host
PATH	This is the colon-separated list of directories where shell will look for commands
PPID	This is the process ID of the shell's parent
PWD	This is the present working directory

More shell variables can be found in man bash.

We will see what values these shell variables contain by printing its value in a shell script:

```
#!/bin/bash
#Filename: builtin_shell_variables.sh
#Description: Knowing about builtin shell variables

echo "My current bash path - $BASH"
echo "Bash version I am using - $BASH_VERSION"
echo "PID of bash I am running - $BASHPID"
echo "My home directory - $HOME"
echo "Where am I currently? - $PWD"
echo "My hostname - $HOSTNAME"
```

After running this script, the output may vary depending upon what the value of these variables is set in your system. The sample output will be as follows:

```
My current bash path - /bin/sh
Bash version I am using - 4.3.33(1)-release
PID of bash I am running - 4549
My home directory - /home/sinny
Where am I currently? - /home/sinny/Documents/
My hostname - localhost.localdomain
```

The shell variables, such as PWD, PATH, HOME, and so on, are very useful and help in getting the information quickly by just echoing a value in it. We can also add or modify the value of some of shell variables, such as PATH, in order to add a custom path in which we want shell to look for commands.

One of the use-cases of modifying the PATH variable value is: suppose, I have compiled a source code that generates a few binaries such as, foo and bar. Now, if I want shell to search in that particular directory for command as well, then add this directory path in the PATH variable and we are done. The following small shell script example shows how to do this:

```
#!/bin/bash
#Filename: path_variable.sh
#Description: Playing with PATH variable

echo "Current PATH variable content - $PATH"
echo "Current directory - $PWD"
echo "Content of current directory\n`ls`"
PATH=$PATH:$PWD
echo "New PATH variable content - $PATH"
# Now execute commands available in current working diectory
```

The output after running this script will be somewhat as follows:

```
Current PATH variable content - /usr/lib64/qt-3.3/bin:/bin:/usr/bin:/
usr/local/bin:/usr/local/sbin:/usr/sbin:/home/sinny/go/source_code/go/
bin:/home/sinny/.local/bin:/home/sinny/bin
Current directory - /home/sinny/test_project/bin
Content of current directory – foo bar
New PATH variable content - /usr/lib64/qt-/usr/lib64/qt-3.3/bin:/
bin:/usr/bin:/usr/local/bin:/usr/local/sbin:/usr/sbin:/home/sinny/
go/source_code/go/bin:/home/sinny/.local/bin:/home/sinny/bin: /home/
sinny/test_project/bin
```

We see from the output that a new PATH variable has my custom path added. From the next time, whenever I run the foo or bar commands with this custom PATH variable set, the absolute path of the foo and the bar command/binary won't be required. Shell will find out these variables by looking into its PATH variable. This is true only during the current session of shell. We will see this in *Chapter 5, Customizing Environment* in recipe, *Modifying a shell environment*.

Operators

Similar to other programming languages, shell programming also supports various types of operators to perform tasks. Operators can be categorized as follows:

- Assignment operator

- Arithmetic operators
- Logical operators
- Comparison operators

The assignment operator

Equal to an operator (=) is the assignment operator that is used to initialize or change the value of a variable. This operator works on any data such as a string, integer, float, array, and so on. For example:

```
$ var=40          # Initializing variable var to integer value
$ var="Hello"     # Changing value of var to string value
$ var=8.9         # Changing value of var to float value
```

Arithmetic operators

Arithmetic operators are used for doing arithmetic operations on integers. They are as follows:

- + (plus)
- - (minus)
- * (multiplication)
- / (division)
- ** (exponentiation)
- % (modulo)
- += (plus-equal)
- -= (minus-equal)
- *= (multiplication-equal)
- /= (slash-equal)
- %= (mod-equal)

To perform any arithmetic operation, we prefix the expr and let keywords before the actual arithmetic expression. The following example shows how to perform an arithmetic operation in bash:

```
#!/bin/bash
#Filename: arithmetic.sh
#Description: Arithmetic evaluation
```

```
num1=10 num2=5
echo "Numbers are num1 = $num1 and num2 = $num2"
echo "Addition = `expr $num1 + $num2`"`"
echo "Subtraction = `expr $num1 - $num2`"
echo "Multiplication = `expr $num1 \* $num2`"
echo "Division = `expr $num1 / $num2`"
let "exponent = $num1 ** num2"
echo "Exponentiation = $exponent"
echo "Modulo = `expr $num1 % $num2`"
let "num1 += $num2"
echo "New num1 = $num1"
let "num1 -= $num1"
echo "New num2 = $num2"
```

The result after running this script will look as follows:

```
Numbers are num1 = 10 and num2 = 5
Addition = 15
Subtraction = 5
Multiplication = 50
Division = 2
Exponentiation = 100000
Modulo = 0
New num1 = 15
New num2 = 5
```

Logical operators

Logical operators are also known as Boolean operators. They are:

! (NOT), && (AND), and || (OR)

Performing a logical operation returns a Boolean value as `true (1)` or `false (0)` depending upon the values of variable(s) on which the operation is done.

One of the useful use-case is: suppose that we want to execute a command if the first command or operation returns successfully. In this case, we can use the `&&` operator. Similarly, if we want to execute another command, irrespective of the first command that got executed or not, then we can use the `||` operator between two commands. We can use the `!` operator to negate the true value. For example:

```
$ cd ~/Documents/ && ls
```

The `cd` command is used to change the current path to the specified argument. Here, the `cd ~/Documents/` command will change the directory to `Documents` if exists. If it fails, then `ls` won't get executed, but if `cd` to `Documents` succeeds, the `ls` command will display the content of `Documents directory`:

```
$ cat ~/file.txt  || echo "Current Working directory $PWD"
cat: /home/skumari/file.txt: No such file or directory
Current Working directory /tmp/
```

The `cat` command displays the content of `file.txt` if it exists. Irrespective of the `cat ~/file.txt` command execution, later the command that is `echo "Current Working directory $PWD"` will be executed:

```
$  ! cd /tmp/foo && mkdir /tmp/foo
bash: cd: /tmp/foo: No such file or directory
```

By running the preceding commands, first it will try to change the directory to `/tmp/foo`. Here, `! cd /tmp/foo` means if change directory to `/tmp/foo` doesn't succeed, then run the second command, which is `mkdir /tmp/foo`. The `mkdir` command is used to create a new directory. As a result of proceeding command execution, directory `/tmp/foo` will be created if it doesn't exist.

```
$ cd /tmp/foo
```

Since the `/tmp/foo` directory has been created, a successful change of the directory will occur.

Comparison operators

Comparison operators compare two variables and check whether a condition is satisfied or not. They are different for integers and strings.

Comparison operators that are valid for integer variables (consider a and b as two integer variables; for example, a=20, b=35) are as follows:

- -eq (is equal to)   - [$a -eq $b]
- -ne (is not equal to)   - [$a -ne $b]
- -gt (is greater than)   - [$a -gt $b]
- -ge or >= (is greater than or equal to) - [$a -ge $b]
- -lt (is less than)   - [$a -lt $b]
- -le (is less than or equal to)   - [$a -le $b]
- < (is less than)   - (($a < $b))

- <= (is less than or equal to)   - (($a <= $b))
- > (is greater than)   - (($a > $b))
- >= (is greater than or equal to)   - (($a >= $b))

Comparison operators that are valid for string variables (consider a and b as two string variables; for example, a="Hello" b="World") are as follows:

- = (is equal to); for example, [$a = $b]
- != (is not equal to); for example, [$a != $b]
- < (is less than); for example, [$a \< $b] or [[$a \< $b]] or (($a \< $b))
- > (is greater than); for example,[$a \> $b] or [[$a > $b]] or (($a \> $b))
- -n (string is non-empty); for example,[-n $a]
- -z (string has zero length or null); for example,[-z $a]

Shell uses the < and > operators for redirection, so it should be used with an escape (\) if used under […]. Double parentheses, ((...)) or [[…]], doesn't need an escape sequence. Using [[…]] also supports pattern matching.

We will see the usage and examples of operators in more detail in *Chapter 3, Effective Script Writing*.

Shell expansions

While working with shell, we perform a lot of similar and repetitive tasks. For example, in the current directory, there are 100 files but we are interested only in shell script whose file extension is .sh. We can execute following command to view only shell script files in current directory:

```
$ ls *.sh
```

This will show all the files ending with .sh. An interesting take away from here is the * wildcard. It means a match list of files whose name can be anything and that ends with .sh.

Shell expands all wildcard patterns. A list of the latest wildcard patterns are as follows:

- ~ (Tilde)
- * (Asterisk)
- ? (Question mark)
- [ ] (Square brackets)
- { } (Curly brackets)

To explain shell expansion for different wildcards, we will create a test folder in our home directory using the mkdir command containing different files mentioned as follows:

```
$ mkdir  ~/test && cd ~/test
$ touch a ab foo bar hello moo foo.c bar.c moo.c hello.txt foo.txt bar.sh
hello.sh moo.sh
```

The touch command creates an empty file if it doesn't exist. If a file exists, then the file timestamp changes:

```
$ ls
a  ab  bar  bar.c  bar.sh  foo  foo.c  foo.txt  hello  hello.sh  hello.
txt  moo  moo.c  moo.sh
```

Running the preceding commands will create a test directory, and inside test directory creates files given as parameter to the touch command.

~ (Tilde)

~ (Tilde) gets expanded by bash when it is present at the beginning of an unquoted string. The expansion depends upon what tilde-prefix is used. Tilde prefixes are characters until the first unquoted (/) slash. Some of the bash expansions are as follows:

- ~: This is the user's home directory; the value is set in the $HOME variable
- ~user_name: This is the home directory of the user's user_name
- ~user_name/file_name: This is the file/directory file_name in the user's user_name home directory
- ~/file_name: This is the file/directory file_name in the home directory that is $HOME/file_name
- ~+: This is the current working directory; the value is set in the $PWD variable
- ~-: This is the old or last working directory; the value is set in the $OLDPWD variable
- ~+/file_name: This is the file/directory file_name in the current directory that is $PWD/file_name
- ~-/file_name: This is the file/directory file_name in the old/last working directory that is $OLDPWD/file_name

* (Asterisk)

It matches zero or more characters. Take a test directory as an example:

- Display all files as follows:

```
$ ls *
a  ab  bar  bar.c  bar.sh  foo  foo.c  foo.txt  hello  hello.sh
hello.txt  moo  moo.c  moo.sh
```

- Display the C source files as follows:

```
$ ls *.c
bar.c  foo.c  moo.c
```

- Display files that have a in its name, as follows:

```
$ ls *a*
a  ab  bar  bar.c  bar.sh
```

- Deleting files with an extension .txt as follows:

```
$ rm *.txt
$ ls
a  ab  bar  bar.c  bar.sh  foo  foo.c  hello  hello.sh  moo  moo.c
moo.sh
```

? (Question mark)

It matches any single character: ? (single question mark will match a single character), ?? (double question mark matches any two characters), and so on. Take a test directory as an example:

```
$ touch a ab foo bar hello moo foo.c bar.c moo.c hello.txt foo.txt bar.sh
hello.sh moo.sh
```

This will recreate files that were removed during the previous example, and also update the access and modification time of the existing files:

- Get files whose name length is irrespective of what the extension file has:

```
$ ls ??
ab
```

- Get files whose name length is 2 or 5:

```
$ ls ?? ?????
ab  bar.c  foo.c  hello  moo.c
```

- Delete files whose name is four characters long:

```
$ rm ????
rm: cannot remove '????': No such file or directory
This error is because there is no file name with 4 character
```

- Move files to the /tmp directory whose name is at least three characters long:

```
$ mv ???* /tmp
$ ls
a ab
```

We see only two files in the test directory because the rest of the files were of the length 3 or more.

[ ] (Square brackets)

Square brackets match any character from the characters mentioned inside the square brackets. Characters can be specified as a word or range.

A range of characters can be specified using - (hyphen). For example:

- [a-c] : This matches a, b, or c
- [a-z] : This matches any character from a to z
- [A-Z] : This matches any character from A to Z
- [0-9] : This matches any character from 0 to 9

Take a test directory as an example and recreate files in a test directory:

```
$ touch a ab foo bar hello moo foo.c bar.c moo.c hello.txt foo.txt bar.sh
hello.sh moo.sh
```

Get files whose name starts with a, b, c, or d with the following command:

```
$ ls [a-d]*
a   ab   bar   bar.c   bar.sh
```

Get files whose name starts with any letter and ends with a letter o or h, with the following command:

```
$ ls [a-zA-Z]*[oh]
foo   hello   hello.sh   moo   moo.sh
```

Get files that have at least the letter o twice in its name, with the following command:

```
$ ls *[o]*[o]*
foo  foo.c  foo.txt  moo  moo.c  moo.sh
```

[!characters] (Exclamation mark) is used to match a character that is not part of a charter set mentioned inside square brackets.

Get files that don't have a number in its name, with the following command:

```
$  ls [!0-9]*
a  ab  bar  bar.c  bar.sh  foo  foo.c  foo.txt  hello  hello.sh  hello.
txt  moo  moo.c  moo.sh
```

{ } (Curly brackets)

It creates multiple wildcard patterns to match. A brace expression may contain either a comma-separated list of strings, a range, or a single character.

A range can be specified by using the following:

- {a..z}: This matches all the charterer from a to z
- {0..6}: This matches numbers 0, 1, 2, 3, 4, 5 and 6

Take a test directory as an example and recreate files in the test directory:

```
$ touch a ab foo bar hello moo foo.c bar.c moo.c hello.txt foo.txt bar.sh
hello.sh moo.sh
```

Get files that have the file extension .sh or .c, with the following command:

```
$ ls {*.sh,*.c}
bar.c  bar.sh  foo.c  hello.sh  moo.c  moo.sh
```

Copy bar.c to bar.html by using the following command:

```
$ cp bar{.c,.cpp}  # Expands to cp bar.c bar.cpp
$ ls bar.*
bar.c  bar.cpp  bar.sh
```

Print the number from 1 to 50 by using the following command:

```
$ echo {1..50}
1 2 3 4 5 6 7 8 9 10 11 12 13 14 15 16 17 18 19 20 21 22 23 24 25 26 27
28 29 30 31 32 33 34 35 36 37 38 39 40 41 42 43 44 45 46 47 48 49 50
```

Create 10 files that start with `hello` and has an extension `.cpp`:

```
$ touch hello{0..9}.cpp
$ ls *.cpp
```

```
hello0.cpp  hello1.cpp  hello2.cpp  hello3.cpp  hello4.cpp  hello5.cpp
hello6.cpp  hello7.cpp  hello8.cpp  hello9.cpp
```

To avoid shell expansion of a wildcard, use backslash (\) or write a string within a single quote (' ').

Construct commands using eval

The `eval` command is a shell builtin command used to construct a command by concatenating arguments passed to `eval`. A concatenated command is further executed by shell and returns a result. If no arguments are given to `eval`, it returns `0`.

The syntax of the `eval` command is as follows:

```
eval [arg ...]
```

The following example shows the expansion of a variable to the name of another variable using `eval`:

```
$ name=foo
$ foo="Welcome to foo world"
$ echo $name
foo
$ new_name='$'$name     #new_name just stores string value $foo
$ echo $new_name
$foo
$ eval new_name='$'$name  # eval processes $foo string into variable
and  prints                # foo variable value
Welcome to foo world
```

Another example where `eval` can be useful is as follows:

```
$ pipe="|"
$  df $pipe wc  # Will give error because
df: '|': No such file or directory
df: 'wc': No such file or directory
$ eval df $pipe wc  # eval executes it as shell command
12      73      705
```

Here, the df command shows a system disk's usage:

```
A shell script showing the use of eval is as follows:
#!/bin/bash
#Filename: eval.sh
#Description: Evaluating string as a command using eval

cmd="ls /usr"
echo "Output of command $cmd -"
eval $cmd    #eval will treat content of cmd as shell command and
execute it
cmd1="ls /usr | wc -l"
echo "Line count of /usr -"
eval $cmd1

expression="expr 2 + 4 \* 6"
echo "Value of $expression"
eval $expression
```

Running the script will give you the following result:

```
Output of command ls /usr -
avr  bin  games  include  lib  lib64  libexec  local  sbin  share  src
tmp
Line count of /usr -
12
Value of expr 2 + 4 \* 6
26
```

Make bash behave using set

The set command is a shell builtin command that is used to set and unset a value of the local variables in shell.

The syntax of using set is as follows:

```
set [--abBCefhHkmnpPtuvx] [-o option] [arg ...]
```

Some of the option values are allexport, braceexpand, history, keyword, verbose, and xtrace.

Using `set` without any option displays the name and value of all shell variables and functions, in a format that can be reused as an input for setting and unsetting the currently set variables.

Exit on the first failure

In a shell script, by default, the next line is executed if an error occurs in the current line. Sometimes, we may want to stop running a script further after an error has been encountered. The `-e` option of `set` ensures to exit a script once any of the commands in a pipeline fails.

In the following shell script, `do_not_exit_on_failure.sh` doesn't use `set` with the option `-e`:

`$ cat do_not_exit_on_failure.sh`

```
#!/bin/bash
# Filename: do_not_exit_on_failure.sh
# Description: Resume script after an error

echo "Before error"
cd /root/        # Will give error
echo "After error"
```

After running this script, the output is as follows:

```
Before error
do_not_exit_on_failure.sh: line 6: cd: /root/: Permission denied
After error
```

We see that the command after the error gets executed as well. In order to stop the execution after an error is encountered, use `set -e` in the script. The following script demonstrates the same:

`$ cat exit_on_failure.sh`

```
#!/bin/bash
# Filename: exit_on_failure.sh
# Description: Exits script after an error

set -e
echo "Before error"
cd /root/        # Will give error
echo "After error"
```

The output after running the preceding script is as follows:

```
Before error
exit_on_failure.sh: line 7: cd: /root/: Permission denied
```

We can see that the script has been terminated after encountering an error at the line number 7.

Enabling/disabling symbolic link's resolution path

Using set with the -P option doesn't resolve symbolic links. Following example demonstrate how we can enable or disable symbolic link resolution of /bin directory which is symbolic link of /usr/bin/ directory:

```
$ ls -l /bin
lrwxrwxrwx. 1 root root 7 Nov 18 18:03 /bin -> usr/bin
$ set -P      # -P enable symbolic link resolution
$ cd /bin
$ pwd
/usr/bin
$ set +P    # Disable symbolic link resolution
$ pwd
/bin
```

Setting/unsetting variables

We can use the set command to see all local variables accessible for the current process. The local variables are not accessible in the subprocess.

We can create our own variable and set it locally as follows:

```
$ MYVAR="Linux Shell Scripting"
$ echo $MYVAR
 Linux Shell Scripting
$ set | grep MYVAR  # MYVAR local variable is created
MYVAR='Linux Shell Scripting'
$ bash     # Creating a new bash sub-process in current bash
$ set | grep MYVAR
$    # Blank because MYVAR is local variable
```

To make a variable accessible to its subprocesses as well, use the `export` command followed by the variable to be exported:

```
$ MYVARIABLE="Hello World"
$ export  MYVARIABLE
$ bash     # Creating a new bash sub-process under bash
$ echo $MYVARIABLE
Hello World
```

This will export the MYVARIABLE variable to any subprocess that ran from that process. To check whether MYVARIABLE has exported or not, run the following command:

```
$ export |grep MYVARIABLE
declare -x MYVARIABLE="Hello World"
$ export | grep MYVAR
$MYVAR variable is not present in sub-process but variable MYVARIABLE is
present in sub-process.
```

To unset local or exported variables, use the `unset` command and it will reset the value of the variable to null:

```
$ unset MYVAR          # Unsets local variable MYVAR
$ unset  MYVARIABLE     # Unsets exported variable MYVARIABLE
```

Summary

After reading this chapter, you understood how to write simple shell script in bash by printing, echoing, and asking user input. You should now have a good understanding of defining and using variables in shell and what builtin shell variables exist. You are now familiar with what operators are available in shell and how they can create and evaluate their own expression. With information about wildcards available in this chapter, it makes work easier for you while you are dealing with similar kind of data or pattern. The shell builtin command `set` enables modifying shell variables easily.

This chapter has built a foundation for upcoming chapters. Now, in next chapter, you will get to know about standard inputs, outputs, and errors. Also, there will be a detailed coverage of how to use an output from commands and then filter/transform them to show the data according to your need.

2
Getting Hands-on with I/O, Redirection Pipes, and Filters

In day-to-day work, we come across different kinds of files such as text files, source code files from different programming languages (for example, `file.sh`, `file.c`, and `file.cpp`), and so on. While working, we often perform various operations on files or directories such as searching for a given string or pattern, replacing strings, printing few lines of a file, and so on. Performing these operations is not easy if we have to do it manually. Manual searching for a string or pattern in a directory having thousands of files can take months, and has high chances of making errors.

Shell provides many powerful commands to make our work easier, faster, and error-free. Shell commands have the ability to manipulate and filter text from different streams such as standard input, file, and so on. Some of these commands are `grep`, `sed`, `head`, `tr`, `sort`, and so on. Shell also comes with a feature of redirecting output from one command to another with the pipe ('|'). Using pipe helps to avoids creation of unnecessary temporary files.

One of the best qualities of these commands is that they come along with the `man` pages. We can directly go to the `man` page and see what all features they provide by running the `man` command. Most of the commands have options such as `--help` to find the help usage and `--version` to know the version number of the command.

This chapter will cover the following topics in detail:

- Standard I/O and error streams
- Redirecting the standard I/O and error streams
- Pipe and pipelines—connecting commands
- Regular expressions

- Filtering output using `grep`
- Editing output using `sed`
- Duplicating a stream using `tee`
- Sorting and finding unique text
- Character-based translation using `tr`
- Filtering based on lines—`head` and `tail`
- Cut-based selection

Standard I/O and error streams

In shell programming, there are different ways to provide an input (for example, via a keyboard and terminal) and display an output (for example, terminal and file) and error (for example, terminal), if any, during the execution of a command or program.

The following examples show the input, output, and error while running the commands:

- The input from a user by a keyboard and the input obtained by a program via a standard input stream, that is terminal, is taken as follows:

```
$ read -p "Enter your name:"
Enter your name:Foo
```

- The output printed on the standard output stream, that is terminal, is as follows:

```
$ echo "Linux Shell Scripting"
Linux Shell Scripting
```

- The error message printed on the standard error stream, that is terminal, is as follows:

```
$ cat hello.txt
cat: hello.txt: No such file or directory
```

When a program executes, by default, three files get opened with it which are `stdin`, `stdout`, and `stderr`. The following table provides a short description of each of these:

File descriptor number	File name	Description
0	stdin	This is standard input being read from the terminal
1	stdout	This is standard output to the terminal
2	stderr	This is standard error to the terminal

File descriptors

File descriptors are integer numbers representing opened files in an operating system. The unique file descriptor numbers are provided to each opened files. File descriptors' numbers go up from 0.

Whenever a new process in Linux is created, then standard input, output, and error files are provided to it along with other needed opened files to process.

To know what all open file descriptors are associated with a process, we will consider the following example:

Run an application and get its process ID first. Consider running bash as an example to get PID of bash:

```
$ pidof bash
2508 2480 2464 2431 1281
```

We see that multiple bash processes are running. Take one of the bash PID example, 2508, and run the following command:

```
$  ls -l /proc/2508/fd
```

```
total 0
lrwx------. 1 sinny sinny 64 May 20 00:03 0 -> /dev/pts/5
lrwx------. 1 sinny sinny 64 May 20 00:03 1 -> /dev/pts/5
lrwx------. 1 sinny sinny 64 May 19 23:22 2 -> /dev/pts/5
lrwx------. 1 sinny sinny 64 May 20 00:03 255 -> /dev/pts/5
```

We see that 0, 1, and 2 opened file descriptors are associated with process bash. Currently, all of them are pointing to /dev/pts/5. pts, which is pseudo terminal slave.

So, whatever we will do in this bash, input, output, and error related to this PID, output will be written to the /dev/pts/5 file. However, the pts files are pseudo files and contents are in memory, so you won't see anything when you open the file.

Redirecting the standard I/O and error streams

We have an option to redirect standard input, output, and errors, for example, to a file, another command, intended stream, and so on. Redirection is useful in different ways. For example, I have a bash script whose output and errors are displayed on a standard output—that is, terminal. We can avoid mixing an error and output by redirecting one of them or both to a file. Different operators are used for redirection. The following table shows some of operators used for redirection, along with its description:

Operator	Description
>	This redirects a standard output to a file
>>	This appends a standard output to a file
<	This redirects a standard input from a file
>&	This redirects a standard output and error to a file
>>&	This appends a standard output and error to a file
|	This redirects an output to another command

Redirecting standard output

An output of a program or command can be redirected to a file. Saving an output to a file can be useful when we have to look into the output in the future. A large number of output files for a program that runs with different inputs can be used in studying program output behavior.

For example, showing redirecting echo output to output.txt is as follows:

```
$ echo "I am redirecting output to a file" > output.txt
$
```

We can see that no output is displayed on the terminal. This is because output was redirected to output.txt. The operator '>' (greater than) tells the shell to redirect the output to whatever filename mentioned after the operator. In our case, it's output.txt:

```
$ cat output.txt
I am redirecting output to a file
```

Now, let's add some more output to the `output.txt` file:

```
$ echo "I am adding another line to file" > output.txt
$ cat output.txt
I am adding another line to file
```

We noticed that the previous content of the `output.txt` file got erased and it only has the latest redirected content. To retain the previous content and append the latest redirected output to a file, use the operator '>>':

```
$ echo "Adding one more line" >> output.txt
$ cat output.txt
I am adding another line to file
Adding one more line
```

We can also redirect an output of a program/command to another command in bash using the operator '|' (pipe):

```
$ ls /usr/lib64/ | grep libc.so
libc.so
libc.so.6
```

In this example, we gave the output of `ls` to the `grep` command using the '|' (pipe) operator, and `grep` gave the matching search result of the `libc.so` library:

Redirecting standard input

Instead of getting an input from a standard input to a command, it can be redirected from a file using the < (less than) operator. For example, we want to count the number of words in the `output.txt` file created from the *Redirecting standard output* section:

```
$ cat  output.txt
I am adding another line to file
Adding one more line
$  wc -w < output.txt
11
```

We can sort the content of `output.txt`:

```
$ sort < output.txt     # Sorting output.txt on stdout
Adding one more line
I am adding another line to file
```

We can also give a `patch` file as an input to the `patch` command in order to apply a `patch.diff` in a source code. The command `patch` is used to apply additional changes made in a file. Additional changes are provided as a `diff` file. A `diff` file contains the changes between the original and the modified file by running the `diff` command. For example, I have a patch file to apply on `output.txt`:

```
$ cat patch.diff     # Content of patch.diff file

2a3
> Testing patch command
$ patch output.txt < patch.diff   # Applying patch.diff to output.txt
$ cat output.txt    # Checking output.txt content after applying patch
I am adding another line to file
Adding one more line
Testing patch command
```

Redirecting standard errors

There is a possibility of getting an error while executing a command/program in bash because of different reasons such as invalid input, insufficient arguments, file not found, bug in program, and so on:

```
$ cd /root  # Doing cd to root directory from a normal user
bash: cd: /root/: Permission denied
Bash prints the error on a terminal saying, permission denied.
```

In general, errors are printed on a terminal so that it's easy for us to know the reason for an error. Printing both the errors and output on the terminal can be annoying because we have to manually look into each line and check whether the program encountered any error:

```
$ cd / ; ls; cat hello.txt; cd /bin/; ls *.{py,sh}
```

We ran a series of commands in the preceding section. First `cd` to `/`, `ls` content of `/`, `cat` file `hello.txt`, `cd` to `/bin` and see files matching `*.py` and `*.sh` in `/bin/`. The output will be as follows:

```
bin  boot  dev  etc  home  lib  lib64  lost+found  media  mnt  opt
proc  root  run  sbin  srv  sys  tmp  usr  var
cat: hello.txt: No such file or directory
alsa-info.sh        kmail_clamav.sh     sb_bnfilter.py  sb_mailsort.py
setup-nsssysinit.sh     amuFormat.sh        kmail_fprot.sh    sb_bnserver.
py     sb_mboxtrain.py     struct2osd.sh       core_server.py  kmail_sav.
sh     sb_chkopts.py       sb_notesfilter.py
```

We see that `hello.txt` doesn't exist in the / directory and because of this there is an error printed on the terminal as well, along with other output. We can redirect the error as follows:

```
$ (cd / ; ls; cat hello.txt; cd /bin/; ls *.{py,sh}) 2> error.txt
```

```
bin   boot   dev   etc   home   lib   lib64   lost+found   media   mnt   opt
proc   root   run   sbin   srv   sys   tmp   usr   var
alsa-info.sh          kmail_clamav.sh      sb_bnfilter.py   sb_mailsort.py
setup-nsssysinit.sh   amuFormat.sh         kmail_fprot.sh   sb_bnserver.
py   sb_mboxtrain.py    struct2osd.sh        core_server.py   kmail_sav.
sh   sb_chkopts.py      sb_notesfilter.py
```

We can see that the error has been redirected to the `error.txt` file. To verify, check the `error.txt` content:

```
$ cat error.txt
```

```
cat: hello.txt: No such file or directory
```

Multiple redirection

We can redirect `stdin`, `stdout`, and `stderr` together in a command or script or a combination of some of them.

The following command redirects both `stdout` and `stder`:

```
$ (ls /home/ ;cat hello.txt;) > log.txt 2>&1
```

Here, `stdout` is redirected to `log.txt` and error messages are redirected to `log.txt` as well. In `2>&1`, `2>` means redirect an error and `&1` means redirect to `stdout`. In our case, we have already redirected `stdout` to the `log.txt` file. So, now both the `stdout` and `stderr` outputs will be written into `log.txt` and nothing will be printed on the terminal. To verify, we will check the content of `log.txt`:

```
$ cat log.txt
```

```
lost+found
```

```
sinny
```

```
cat: hello.txt: No such file or directory
```

The following example shows the `stdin`, `stdout`, and `stderr` redirection:

```
$  cat < ~/.bashrc > out.txt 2> err.txt
```

Here, the `.bashrc` file present in the home directory acts as an input to the `cat` command and its output is redirected to the `out.txt` file. Any error encountered in between is redirected to the `err.txt` file.

The following `bash` script will explain `stdin`, `stdout`, `stderr`, and their redirection with even more clarity:

```
#!/bin/bash
# Filename: redirection.sh
# Description: Illustrating standard input, output, error
# and redirecting them

ps -A -o pid -o command > p_snapshot1.txt
echo -n "Running process count at snapshot1: "
wc -l < p_snapshot1.txt
echo -n "Create a new process with pid = "
tail -f /dev/null &  echo $!    # Creating a new process
echo -n "Running process count at snapshot2: "
ps -A -o pid -o command > p_snapshot2.txt
wc -l < p_snapshot2.txt
echo
echo "Diff bewteen two snapshot:"
diff p_snapshot1.txt p_snapshot2.txt
```

This script saves two snapshots of all running processes in the system and generates `diff`. The output after running the process will look somewhat as follows:

$ sh redirection.sh

```
Running process count at snapshot1: 246
Create a new process with pid = 23874
Running process count at snapshot2: 247

Diff bewteen two snapshot:
246c246,247
< 23872 ps -A -o pid -o command
---
> 23874 tail -f /dev/null
> 23875 ps -A -o pid -o command
```

Pipe and pipelines – connecting commands

The outputs of the programs are generally saved in files for further use. Sometimes, temporary files are created in order to use an output of a program as an input to another program. We can avoid creating temporary files and feed the output of a program as an input to another program using bash pipe and pipelines.

Pipe

The pipe denoted by the operator | connects the standard output of a process in the left to the standard input in the right process by inter process communication mechanism. In other words, the | (pipe) connects commands by providing the output of a command as the input to another command.

Consider the following example:

```
$ cat /proc/cpuinfo | less
```

Here, the cat command, instead of displaying the content of the /proc/cpuinfo file on stdout, passes its output as an input to the less command. The less command takes the input from cat and displays on the stdout per page.

Another example using pipe is as follows:

```
$ ps -aux | wc -l    # Showing number of currently running processes in
system
254
```

Pipeline

Pipeline is a sequence of programs/commands separated by the operator ' | ' where the output of execution of each command is given as an input to the next command. Each command in a pipeline is executed in a new subshell. The syntax will be as follows:

```
command1 | command2 | command3 ...
```

Examples showing pipeline are as follows:

```
$ ls /usr/lib64/*.so | grep libc | wc -l
13
```

Here, we are first getting a list of files from the `/usr/lib64` directory that has the
`.so` extension. The output obtained is passed as an input to the next `grep` command
to look for the `libc` string. The output is further given to the `wc` command to count
the number of lines.

Regular expressions

Regular expression (also known as regex or regexp) provides a way of specifying a
pattern to be matched in a given big chunk of text data. It supports a set of characters
to specify the pattern. It is widely used for a text search and string manipulation. A
lot of shell commands provide an option to specify regex such as `grep`, `sed`, `find`,
and so on.

The regular expression concept is also used in other programming languages such as
C++, Python, Java, Perl, and so on. Libraries are available in different languages to
support regular expression's features.

Regular expression metacharacters

The metacharacters used in regular expressions are explained in the following table:

Metacharacters	Description
* (Asterisk)	This matches zero or more occurrences of the previous character
+ (Plus)	This matches one or more occurrences of the previous character
?	This matches zero or one occurrence of the previous element
. (Dot)	This matches any one character
^	This matches the start of the line
$	This matches the end of line
[...]	This matches any one character within a square bracket
[^...]	This matches any one character that is not within a square bracket
| (Bar)	This matches either the left side or the right side element of |
\{X\}	This matches exactly X occurrences of the previous element
\{X,\}	This matches X or more occurrences of the previous element
\{X,Y\}	This matches X to Y occurrences of the previous element
\(...\)	This groups all the elements
\<	This matches the empty string at the beginning of a word
\>	This matches the empty string at the end of a word
\	This disables the special meaning of the next character

Character ranges and classes

When we look into a human readable file or data, its major content contains alphabets (a to z) and numbers (0 to 9). While writing regex for matching a pattern consisting of alphabets or numbers, we can make use character ranges or classes.

Character ranges

We can use character ranges in a regular expression as well. We can specify a range by a pair of characters separated by a hyphen. Any characters that fall in between that range, inclusive, are matched. Character ranges are enclosed inside square brackets.

The following table shows some of character ranges:

Character range	Description
[a-z]	This matches any single lowercase letter from a to z
[A-Z]	This matches any single uppercase letter from A to Z
[0-9]	This matches any single digit from 0 to 9
[a-zA-Z0-9]	This matches any single alphabetic or numeric characters
[h-k]	This matches any single letter from h to k
[2-46-8j-lB-M]	This matches any single digit from 2 to 4 or 6 to 8 or any letter from j to l or B to M

Character classes: Another way of specifying a range of character matches is by using Character classes. It is specified within the square brackets [:class:]. The possible class value is mentioned in the following table:

Character Class	Description
[:alnum:]	This matches any single alphabetic or numeric character; for example, [a-zA-Z0-9]
[:alpha:]	This matches any single alphabetic character; for example, [a-zA-Z]
[:digit:]	This matches any single digit; for example, [0-9]
[:lower:]	This matches any single lowercase alphabet; for example, [a-z]
[:upper:]	This matches any single uppercase alphabet; for example, [A-Z]
[:blank:]	This matches a space or tab
[:graph:]	This matches a character in the range of ASCII — for example 33-126 — excluding a space character
[:print:]	This matches a character in the range of ASCII — for example. 32-126 — including a space character

Character Class	Description
[:punct:]	This matches any punctuation marks such as '?', '!', '.', ',', and so on
[:xdigit:]	This matches any hexadecimal characters; for example, [a-fA-F0-9]
[:cntrl:]	This matches any control characters

Creating your own regex: In the previous sections of regular expression, we discussed about metacharacters, character ranges, character class, and their usage. Using these concepts, we can create powerful regex that can be used to filter out text data as per our need. Now, we will create a few regex using the concepts we have learned.

Matching dates in mm-dd-yyyy format

We will consider our valid date starting from UNIX Epoch — that is, 1st January 1970. In this example, we will consider all the dates between UNIX Epoch and 30th December 2099 as valid dates. An explanation of forming its regex is given in the following subsections:

Matching a valid month

- 0[1-9] matches 01st to 09th month
- 1[0-2] matches 10th, 11th, and 12th month
- '|' matches either left or right expression

Putting it all together, the regex for matching a valid month of date will be **0[1-9]|1[0-2]**.

Matching a valid day

- 0[1-9] matches 01st to 09th day
- [12][0-9] matches 10th to 29th day
- 3[0-1] matches 30th to 31st day
- '|' matches either left or right expression
- **0[1-9]|[12][0-9]|3[0-1]** matches all the valid days in a date

Matching the valid year in a date

- 19[7-9][[0-9] matches years from 1970 to 1999
- 20[0-9]{2} matches years from 2000 to 2099
- '|' matches either left or right expression
- **19[7-9][0-9]|20[0-9]{2}** matches all the valid years between 1970 to 2099

Combining valid months, days, and years regex to form valid dates

Our date will be in mm-dd-yyyy format. By putting together regex formed in the preceding sections for months, days, and years, we will get regex for the valid date:

(0[1-9] | 1[0-2])-(0[1-9] | [12][0-9] | 3[0-1])-(19[7-9][0-9] | 20[0-9]{2})

There is a nice website, `http://regexr.com/`, where you can also validate regular expression. The following screenshot shows the matching of the valid date among the given input:

Regex for a valid shell variable

In *Chapter 1*, *Beginning of Scripting Journey*, we learned nomenclature of variables in shell. A valid variable name can contain a character from alphanumeric and underscore, and the first letter of the variable can't be a digit.

Keeping these rules in mind, a valid shell variable regex can be written as follows:

^[_a-zA-Z][_a-zA-Z0-9]*$

Here, ^ (caret) matches the start of a line.

The regex [_a-zA-Z] matches _ or any upper or lower case alphabet [_a-zA-Z0-9]* matches zero or multiple occurrences of _,any digit or upper and lower case alphabet $ (Dollar) matches the end of the line.

In character class format, we can write regex as **^[_[:alpha:]][_[:alnum:]]*$**.

The following screenshot shows valid shell variables using regex formed:

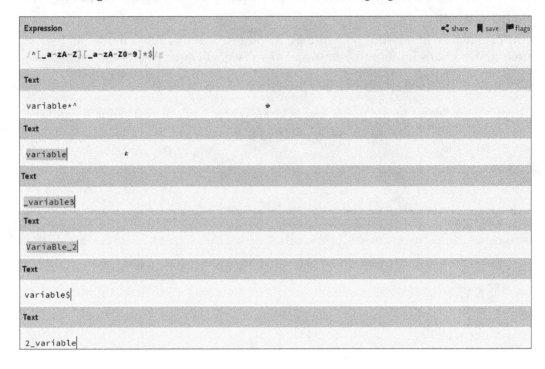

- Enclose regular expression in single quotes (') to avoid pre-shell expansion.
- Use back slash (\) before a character to escape the special meaning of metacharacters.
- Metacharacters such as ?, +, {, |, (, and) are known to be extended regex. They lose their special meaning when used in basic regex. To avoid this, use them with backslash '\?', '\+', '\{', '\|', '\(', and '\)'.

Filtering an output using grep

One of the powerful and widely used command in shell is grep. It searches in an input file and matches lines in which the given pattern is found. By default, all the matched patterns are printed on stdout that is usually terminal. We can also redirect the matched output to other streams such as file. Instead of giving an input from a file, grep can also take the input from the redirected output of the command executed on the left-hand side of '|'.

Syntax

The syntax of using the `grep` command is as follows:

```
grep [OPTIONS] PATTERN [FILE...]
```

Here, FILE can be multiple files for a search. If no file is given as an input for a search, it will search the standard input.

PATTERN can be any valid regular expression. Put PATTERN within single quotes (') or double quotes (") as per need. For example, use single quotes (') to avoid any bash expansion and double quotes (") for expansion.

A lot of OPTIONS are available in `grep`. Some of the important and widely used options are discussed in the following table:

Option	Usage
-i	This enforces case insensitive match in both pattern and input file(s)
-v	This displays the non-matching line
-o	This displays only the matched part in the matching line
-f FILE	This obtains a pattern from a file, one per line
-e PATTERN	This specifies multiple search pattern
-E	This considers pattern as an extended regex (egrp)
-r	This reads all the files in a directory recursively, excluding resolving of symbolic links unless explicitly specified as an input file
-R	This reads all the files in a directory recursively and resolving symbolic if any
-a	This processes binary file as a text file
-n	This prefixes each matched line along with a line number
-q	Don't print anything on stdout
-s	Don't print error messages
-c	This prints the count of matching lines of each input file
-A NUM	This prints NUM lines after the actual string match. (No effect with the -o option)
-B NUM	This prints NUM lines before the actual string match. (No effect with the -o option)
-C NUM	This prints NUM lines after and before the actual string match. (No effect with the -o option)

Looking for a pattern in a file

A lot of times we have to search for a given string or a pattern in a file. The `grep` command provides us the capability to do it in a single line. Let's see the following example:

The input file for our example will be `input1.txt`:

```
$ cat input1.txt  # Input file for our example

    This file is a text file to show demonstration
    of grep command. grep is a very important and
    powerful command in shell.
    This file has been used in chapter 2
```

We will try to get the following information from the `input1.txt` file using the `grep` command:

- Number of lines
- Line starting with a capital letter
- Line ending with a period (.)
- Number of sentences
- Searching sub-string `sent  lines` that don't have a `period`Number of times the string `file` is used

The following shell script demonstrates how to do the above mentioned tasks:

```
#!/bin/bash
#Filename: pattern_search.sh
#Description: Searching for a pattern using input1.txt file

echo "Number of lines = `grep -c '.*' input1.txt`"
echo "Line starting with capital letter:"
grep -c ^[A-Z].* input1.txt
echo
echo "Line ending with full stop (.):"
grep '.*\.$' input1.txt
echo
echo -n "Number of sentence = "
grep -c '\.' input1.txt
echo "Strings matching sub-string sent:"
grep -o "sent" input1.txt
echo
echo "Lines not having full stop are:"
grep -v '\.' input1.txt
echo
echo -n "Number of times string file used: = "
grep -o "file" input1.txt | wc -w
```

The output after running the `pattern_search.sh` shell script will be as follows:

```
Number of lines = 4
Line starting with capital letter:
2

Line ending with full stop (.):
powerful command in shell.

Number of sentence = 2
Strings matching sub-string sent:

Lines not having full stop are:
This file is a text file to show demonstration
This file has been used in chapter 2

Number of times string file used: = 3
```

Looking for a pattern in multiple files

The `grep` command also allows us to search for a pattern in multiple files as an input. To explain this in detail, we will head directly to the following example:

The input files, in our case, will be `input1.txt` and `input2.txt`.

We will reuse the content of the `input1.txt` file from the previous example:

The content of `input2.txt` is as follows:

```
$ cat input2.txt

    Another file for demonstrating grep CommaNd usage.
    It allows us to do CASE Insensitive string test
    as well.
    We can also do recursive SEARCH in a directory
    using -R and -r Options.
    grep allows to give a regular expression to
    search for a PATTERN.
    Some special characters like . * ( ) { } $ ^ ?
    are used to form regexp.
    Range of digit can be given to regexp e.g. [3-6],
    [7-9], [0-9]
```

We will try to get the following information from the `input1.txt` and `input2.txt` files using the `grep` command:

- Search for the string `command`
- Case-insensitive search of the string `command`
- Print the line number where the string `grep` matches
- Search for punctuation marks
- Print one line followed by the matching lines while searching for the string `important`

The following shell script demonstrates how to follow the preceding steps:

```
#!/bin/bash
# Filename: multiple_file_search.sh
# Description: Demonstrating search in multiple input files

echo "This program searches in files input1.txt and input2.txt"
echo "Search result for string \"command\":"
grep "command" input1.txt input2.txt
echo
echo "Case insensitive search of string \"command\":"
# input{1,2}.txt will be expanded by bash to input1.txt input2.txt
grep -i "command" input{1,2}.txt
echo
echo "Search for string \"grep\" and print matching line too:"
grep -n "grep" input{1,2}.txt
echo
echo "Punctuation marks in files:"
grep -n [[:punct:]] input{1,2}.txt
echo
echo "Next line content whose previous line has string \"important\":"
grep -A 1 'important' input1.txt input2.txt
```

The following screenshot is the output after running the shell script `pattern_search.sh`. The matched pattern string has been highlighted:

```
This program searches in files input1.txt and input2.txt
Search result for string "command":
input1.txt:of grep command. grep is a very important and
input1.txt:powerful command in shell.

Case insensitive search of string "command":
input1.txt:of grep command. grep is a very important and
input1.txt:powerful command in shell.
input2.txt:Another file for demonstrating grep CommaNd usage.

Search for string "grep" and print matching line too:
input1.txt:2:of grep command. grep is a very important and
input2.txt:1:Another file for demonstrating grep CommaNd usage.
input2.txt:6:grep allows to give a regular expression to

Punctuation marks in files:
input1.txt:2:of grep command. grep is a very important and
input1.txt:3:powerful command in shell.
input2.txt:1:Another file for demonstrating grep CommaNd usage.
input2.txt:3:as well.
input2.txt:5:using -R and -r Options.
input2.txt:7:search for a PATTERN.
input2.txt:8:Some special characeters like . * ( ) { } $ ^ ?
input2.txt:9:are used to form regexp.
input2.txt:10:Range of digit can be given to regexp e.g. [3-6],
input2.txt:11:[7-9], [0-9]

Next line content whose previous line has string "important":
input1.txt:of grep command. grep is a very important and
input1.txt powerful command in shell.
```

A few more grep usages

The following subsections will cover a few more usages of the grep command.

Searching in a binary file

So far, we have seen all the grep examples running on text files. We can also search for a pattern in binary files using grep. For this, we have to tell the grep command to treat a binary file as a text file too. The option -a or –text tells grep to consider a binary file as a test file.

We know that the grep command itself is a binary file that executes and gives a search result.

One of the option in `grep` is `--text`. The string `--text` should be somewhere available in the `grep` binary file. Let's search for it as follows:

```
$ grep --text '\-\-text' /usr/bin/grep
 -a, --text                    equivalent to –binary-files=text
```

We saw that the string `--text` is found in the search path `/usr/bin/grep`. The character backslash ('`\`') is used to escape its special meaning.

Now, let's search for the `-w` string in the `wc` binary. We know that the `wc` command has an option `-w` that counts the number of words in an input text.

```
$ grep -a '\-w' /usr/bin/wc
 -w, --words            print the word counts
```

Searching in a directory

We can also tell `grep` to search into all files/directories in a directory recursively using the option `-R`. This avoids the hassle of specifying each file as an input text file to `grep`.

For example, we are interested in knowing at how many places `#include <stdio.h>` is used in a standard `include` directory:

```
$ grep -R '\#include <stdio\.h>' /usr/include/ | wc -l
77
```

This means that the `#include <stdio.h>` string is found at `77` places in the `/usr/include` directory.

In another example, we want to know how many Python files (the extension `.py`) in `/usr/lib64/python2.7/` does `"import os"`. We can check that as follows:

```
$ grep -R "import os" /usr/lib64/python2.7/*.py | wc -l
93
```

Excluding files/directories from a search

We can also specify the `grep` command to exclude a particular directory or file from search. This is useful when we don't want `grep` to look into a file or directory that has some confidential information. This is also useful in the case where we are sure that searching into a certain directory will be of no use. So, excluding them will reduce search time.

Suppose, there is a source code directory called s0, which uses the git version control. Now, we are interested in searching for a text or pattern in source files. In this case, searching in the .git subdirectory will be of no use. We can exclude .git from search as follows:

```
$ grep -R --exclude-dir=.git "search_string" s0
```

Here, we are searching for the search_string string in the s0 directory and telling grep to not to search in the .git directory.

Instead of excluding a directory, to exclude a file, use the --exclude-from=FILE option.

Display a filename with a matching pattern

In some use-case, we don't bother with where the search matched and at how many places the search matched in a file. Instead, we are interested in knowing only the filename where at least one search matched.

For example, I want to save filenames that have a particular search pattern found in a file, or redirect to some other command for further processing. We can achieve this using the -l option:

```
$ grep -Rl "import os" /usr/lib64/python2.7/*.py > search_result.txt
$ wc -l search_result.txt

    79
```

This example gets name of the file in which import os is written and saves result in file search_result.txt.

Matching an exact word

The exact matching of the word is also possible using word boundary that is \b on both the sides of the search pattern.

Here, we will reuse the input1.txt file and its content:

```
$ grep -i --color "\ba\b" input1.txt
```

The --color option allows colored printing of the matched search result.

The "\ba\b" option tells grep to only look for the character **a** that is alone. In search results, it won't match the character a present as a sub-string in a string.

The following screenshot shows the output:

```
This file is a text file to show demonstration
of grep command. grep is a very important and
```

Editing output using sed

The `sed` command is a non-interactive stream editor that allows you to modify the content of the standard input or file. It performs an operation on each line in a pipeline. The syntax will be:

```
sed [OPTIONS]... {script} [input-file …]
```

By default, the output is displayed on `stdout`, but can be redirected to a file if specified.

The `input-file` are the files on which `sed` needs to be run. If no files are specified, it reads from `stdin`.

The `script` can be a command or a file with multiple commands to pass to `sed`, and `OPTIONS` to `sed` are described in the following table:

Option	Description
-n	This suppresses automatic printing of pattern space
-e script	This allows multiple scripts to be executed
-r	This uses the extended regex in the script
-l N	This specifies line wrap length
--posix	This disables all GNU extensions
-u	This loads the minimal amounts of data from input and flushes output buffers frequently

String substitution using s

The `sed` command is widely used for string substitution in a text file. Programmers frequently use this feature while renaming a variable in a huge source code. It saves a lot of programmers' time by avoiding manual renaming.

The substitution command `s` has the following field:

```
s/regex/replacement/
```

Here, s means perform substitution, / acts as separator, and `regex` is a regular expression that needs to be replaced. A simple string can also be specified here. The last field `replacement` is with what matched results should be replaced.

By default, `sed` will replace only the first occurrence of a matched pattern in a line. To replace all occurrences, use the `g` flag after the end of /−, that is, `s/regex/replacement/g`.

Some of the flags that can be used are mentioned in the following table:

Flag	Description
g	This applies replacement to all the matches in a line
p	This prints a new pattern space, if substitution occurs
w filename	This writes substituted pattern space to a filename
N	This replaces only the Nth matched result in a matched line

We have the `sed.sh` file for our example. The content of this file is as follows:

$ cat sed.sh

```
#!/bin/bash

var1="sed "
var1+="command "
var1+="usage"

echo $var1
```

This is a shell script, where the variable `var1` has been used at four places. Now, we want to rename the variable `var1` to `variable`. We can do this very easily using the `sed` command:

$ sed -i 's/var1/variable/g' sed.sh
$ cat sed.sh

```
#!/bin/bash

variable="sed "
variable+="command "
variable+="usage"

echo $variable
```

Here, the `-i` option is used to replace an input file.

Multiple substitutions

We can also specify multiple commands to be executed for substitution using `-e` followed by a command.

For example, consider the `sed.txt` file. The content of this file is as follows:

```
$ cat sed.txt
The sed command is widely used for string
substitution in text file. Programmers frequently
use this feature while renaming a variable in huge source code.
It saves lot of programmers time by avoiding manual renaming.
```

Now, we want to replace '.' with ',' and delete the line containing a string `manual`:

```
$ sed -e 's/\./,/g' -e '/manual/d' sed.txt
The sed command is widely used for string
substitution in text file, Programmers frequently
use this feature while renaming a variable in huge source code,
```

In `sed.txt` file, the `s/\./,/g` command first replaces '.' with ',' and `/manual/d` deletes further the line containing the string `manual`.

Duplicating a stream using tee

In some cases, it's necessary to print an output on `stdout` and save an output in a file. In general, command output can either be printed or can be saved in a file. To solve it, the `tee` command is used. This command reads from the standard input and writes to both standard output and files. The syntax of `tee` will be as follows:

```
tee [OPTION] [FILE ...]
```

The `tee` command copies the output to each `FILE` and also to `stdout`. The `OPTIONS` can be as follows:

Option	Description
`-a, --append`	This appends to the `FILE` instead of overwriting
`-i, --ignore-interrupts`	This ignores interrupt signals, if any

Writing an output to stdout and file: In general, to write an output to stdout and file, we will call the same command twice, with and without redirection. For example, the following command shows how to print an output on stdout and save it to a file:

```
$  ls /usr/bin/*.pl  # Prints output on stdout
/usr/bin/rsyslog-recover-qi.pl  /usr/bin/syncqt.pl
$  ls /usr/bin/*.pl> out.txt    # Saves output in file out.txt
```

We can do both the tasks by running the ls command once using the tee command as follows:

```
$  ls /usr/bin/*.pl| tee  out.txt    # Output gets printed to stdout and
saved in out.txt
/usr/bin/rsyslog-recover-qi.pl
/usr/bin/syncqt.pl
$ cat out.txt        #Checking content of out.txt
/usr/bin/rsyslog-recover-qi.pl
/usr/bin/syncqt.pl
```

We can also specify multiple filenames to tee for an output to be written in each file. This copies the output to all files:

```
$ ls /usr/bin/*.pl| tee  out1.txt out2.txt
/usr/bin/rsyslog-recover-qi.pl
/usr/bin/syncqt.pl
```

By running the above commands, the output will be also written to the out1.txt and out2.txt files:

```
$ cat out1.txt
/usr/bin/rsyslog-recover-qi.pl
/usr/bin/syncqt.pl
$ cat out2.txt
/usr/bin/rsyslog-recover-qi.pl
/usr/bin/syncqt.pl
```

Writing an output to stdout and appending to a file

The `tee` command also allows you to append the output to a file instead of overwriting a file. This can be done using the `-a` option with `tee`. Appending an output to a file is useful when we want to write an output of various commands or an error log of different command execution in a single file.

For example, if we want to keep the output of running the `ls` and `echo` commands in the `out3.txt` file and also display results on `stdout`, we can do as follows:

```
$ echo "List of perl file in /usr/bin/ directory" | tee out3.txt
List of perl file in /usr/bin/ directory


$ ls /usr/bin/*.pl| tee  -a out3.txt
/usr/bin/rsyslog-recover-qi.pl
/usr/bin/syncqt.pl


$ cat out3.txt    # Content of file
List of perl file in /usr/bin/ directory
/usr/bin/rsyslog-recover-qi.pl
/usr/bin/syncqt.pl
```

Sending an output to multiple commands

We can also use the `tee` command to provide an output of a command as an input to multiple commands. This is done by sending the `tee` output to pipe:

```
$ df -h | tee out4.txt | grep tmpfs | wc -l
7
```

Here, the output of the `df -h` command is saved to the `out4.txt` file, the `stdout` output is redirected to the `grep` command, and the output of the search result from `grep` is further redirected to the `wc` command. At the end, the result of `wc` is printed on `stdout`.

Sorting and finding unique text

Shell provides different ways to sort the input text using the `sort` command. It's also possible to remove repeated lines from sorted/unsorted input text using the `uniq` command. The input text to sort and `uniq` commands can be given from a file, or redirected from another command.

Sorting an input text

The lines in the input text are sorted in the following order:

- Numbers from 0 to 9
- Uppercase letters from A to Z
- Lowercase letters from a to z

The syntax will be as follows:

```
sort [OPTION] [FILE ...]
```

Single or multiple input files can be provided to sort for sorting.

The `sort` command takes multiple options to provide flexibility in sorting. The popular and important OPTION to sort have been discussed in the following table:

Option	Description
`-b`	This ignores leading blanks
`-d`	This considers only blanks and alphanumeric characters
`-f`	This ignores a case
`-i`	This ignores a non-printable character
`-M`	This compares months that are unknown (for example, < JAN < FEB... < DEC)
`-n`	This sorts on the basis of numerical values
`-r`	This sorts in reverse order
`-h`	This sorts on human-readable numbers; for example, 9K, 5M, 1G, and so on.
`-u`	This gets unique lines
`-o file`	This writes an output to a file instead of stdout
`-m`	This merges the already sorted file without resorting it
`-k n`	This sorts data according to the given column n

Now, we will see with the help of examples, how different sorting can be done on the input text data.

Sorting a single file

In our example, we will consider the `sort1.txt` file for sorting. The content of this file is as follows:

```
$ cat sort1.txt
Japan
Singapore
Germany
Italy
France
Sri Lanka
```

To sort the content alphabetically, we can use the `sort` command without any option:

```
$ sort sort1.txt
France
Germany
Italy
Japan
Singapore
Sri Lanka
```

To sort the content in reverse order, we can use the `-r` option:

```
$ sort -r sort1.txt
Sri Lanka
Singapore
Japan
Italy
Germany
France
```

Sorting multiple files: We can also sort multiple files collectively, and the sorted output can be used for further queries.

For example, consider `sort1.txt` and `sort2.txt` files. We will reuse the content of the `sort1.txt` file from the previous example. The content of `sort2.txt` is as follows:

```
$ cat sort2.txt
India
USA
Canada
China
Australia
```

We can sort both the files together alphabetically as follows:

```
$ sort sort1.txt sort2.txt
Australia
Canada
China
France
Germany
India
Italy
Japan
Singapore
Sri Lanka
USA
```

We can also use the `-o` option to save the sorted output of files in a file instead of displaying it on `stdout`:

```
$ sort sort1.txt sort2.txt -o sorted.txt
$ cat sorted.txt
Australia
Canada
China
France
Germany
India
Italy
Japan
Singapore
Sri Lanka
USA
```

Redirecting output to sort

We can sort an output redirected from another command. The following example shows the sorting of the `df -h` command output:

```
$ df -h      #  Disk space usage in human readable format
```

```
Filesystem        Size   Used  Avail Use% Mounted on
devtmpfs          3.9G      0   3.9G   0% /dev
tmpfs             3.9G   120K   3.9G   1% /dev/shm
tmpfs             3.9G  1020K   3.9G   1% /run
tmpfs             3.9G      0   3.9G   0% /sys/fs/cgroup
/dev/sda2          50G    13G    34G  28% /
tmpfs             3.9G   248K   3.9G   1% /tmp
/dev/sda1         477M   245M   203M  55% /boot
/dev/sda6         102G    70G    32G  69% /media/Data
/dev/dm-0         140G   115G    18G  87% /home
tmpfs             787M      0   787M   0% /run/user/989
tmpfs             787M    28K   787M   1% /run/user/1000
```

The following command sorts output of `df` by its 2nd column content:

```
$ df -h | sort -hb -k2  #. Sorts by 2nd column according to size available:
```

```
Filesystem        Size   Used  Avail Use% Mounted on
/dev/sda1         477M   245M   203M  55% /boot
tmpfs             787M      0   787M   0% /run/user/989
tmpfs             787M    28K   787M   1% /run/user/1000
devtmpfs          3.9G      0   3.9G   0% /dev
tmpfs             3.9G      0   3.9G   0% /sys/fs/cgroup
tmpfs             3.9G   1.0M   3.9G   1% /run
tmpfs             3.9G   120K   3.9G   1% /dev/shm
tmpfs             3.9G   516K   3.9G   1% /tmp
/dev/sda2          50G    13G    34G  28% /
/dev/sda6         102G    70G    32G  69% /media/Data
/dev/dm-0         140G   115G    18G  87% /home
```

We can sort the `ls -l` output according to the last modification day and month:

```
$ ls -l /var/cache/    # Long listing content of /var/cache
```

```
total 64
drwxrwxr-x.  2 abrt  abrt   4096 Feb 24 20:40 abrt-di
drwxr-xr-x.  5 root  root   4096 Mar 12 12:15 app-info
drwxrws---.  2 root  ccache 4096 Oct 20  2014 ccache
drwxrwx---.  3 root  lp     4096 Jun  5 01:37 cups
drwxr-xr-x.  3 root  root   4096 Dec 12 19:19 dnf
drwxr-xr-x.  2 root  root   4096 Jun  5 10:25 fontconfig
drwxr-xr-x.  2 root  root   4096 Dec  1  2014 foomatic
drwxr-xr-x.  2 root  root   4096 Apr 15 18:06 krb5rcache
drwx------.  2 root  root   4096 Jun  5 10:31 ldconfig
drwx--x--x.  3 root  root   4096 Apr 28 21:36 libvirt
drwxr-sr-x. 37 root  man    4096 Jun  6 11:47 man
drwxrwsr-x.  3 root  mock   4096 May 14 03:00 mock
drwxr-xr-x.  5 root  root   4096 Jan 19 23:56 PackageKit
drwxr-xr-x.  2 root  root   4096 May  6 19:04 powertop
drwxr-xr-x.  2 root  root   4096 Apr 14 16:43 realmd
drwxrwxr-x.  3 root  root   4096 Dec 12 19:13 yum
```

To sort the `ls -l` output, first sort according to the month that is the 6th field using the `-M` option, and if the month for two or more row is the same, then sort according to the day that is the 7th field using `-n` for numerical sort:

`$ ls -l /var/cache/ | sort -bk 6M -nk7`

```
total 64
drwxr-xr-x.  5 root  root   4096 Jan 19 23:56 PackageKit
drwxrwxr-x.  2 abrt  abrt   4096 Feb 24 20:40 abrt-di
drwxr-xr-x.  5 root  root   4096 Mar 12 12:15 app-info
drwxr-xr-x.  2 root  root   4096 Apr 14 16:43 realmd
drwxr-xr-x.  2 root  root   4096 Apr 15 18:06 krb5rcache
drwx--x--x.  3 root  root   4096 Apr 28 21:36 libvirt
drwxr-xr-x.  2 root  root   4096 May  6 19:04 powertop
drwxrwsr-x.  3 root  mock   4096 May 14 03:00 mock
drwxrwx---.  3 root  lp     4096 Jun  5 01:37 cups
drwxr-xr-x.  2 root  root   4096 Jun  5 10:25 fontconfig
drwx------.  2 root  root   4096 Jun  5 10:31 ldconfig
drwxr-sr-x. 37 root  man    4096 Jun  6 11:47 man
drwxrws---.  2 root  ccache 4096 Oct 20  2014 ccache
drwxr-xr-x.  2 root  root   4096 Dec  1  2014 foomatic
drwxr-xr-x.  3 root  root   4096 Dec 12 19:19 dnf
drwxrwxr-x.  3 root  root   4096 Dec 12 19:13 yum
```

Filtering unique elements

In many use-case, we need to remove duplicate items and keep only one occurrence of items. It is very useful when the output of a command or input file is too big, and it contains lot of duplicate lines. To get unique lines from a file or redirected output, the shell command `uniq` is used. One important point to note is that, in order to get the `uniq` output, input should be sorted, or first run the sort command to make it sorted. The syntax will be as follows:

```
sort [OPTION] [INPUT [OUTPUT]]
```

An input to `uniq` can be given from a file or another command's output.

If an input file is provided, then an optional output file can also be specified on a command line. If no output file is specified, the output will be printed on `stdout`.

The options that `uniq` supports are discussed in the following table:

Option	Description
-c	This prefixes lines with the number of occurrences
-d	This prints duplicate lines only once
-f N	This skips the comparison of the first N fields
-i	This is case-insensitive comparison of items
-u	This prints only unique lines
-s N	This avoids comparing the first N characters in line
-w N	This compares only N characters in line

Unique elements in a file

Consider the `unique.txt` file as an example on which we will run the `uniq` command with its options. The content of `unique.txt` is as follows:

```
$ cat unique.txt
Welcome to Linux shell scripting
1
Welcome to LINUX shell sCripting
2
Welcome To Linux Shell Scripting
4
2
1
Welcome to Linux shell scripting
```

```
2
3
Welcome to Linux shell scripting
2
Welcome to Linux shell scripting
Welcome to LINUX shell sCripting
```

To remove duplicate lines from the `unique.txt` file, we can do the following:

- Firstly, sort the file and then redirect the sorted text to the `uniq` command:

  ```
  $ sort unique.txt | uniq
  ```

- Use the `-u` option with the `sort` command:

  ```
  $ sort  -u unique.txt
  ```

The output from running either of the commands will be the same, as follows:

```
1
2
3
4
Welcome to Linux shell scripting
Welcome to LINUX shell sCripting
Welcome To Linux Shell Scripting
```

We can use the `-c` option to print the number of occurrences of each line in the input file:

```
$ sort unique.txt | uniq -c
```

```
1 1
4 2
1 3
2 4
4 Welcome to Linux shell scripting
2 Welcome to LINUX shell sCripting
1 Welcome To Linux Shell Scripting
```

Using the options -c and -i will print the uniq lines along with the occurrence count. A comparison for unique line will be done case-insensitive:

```
$ sort unique.txt | uniq -ci
```

```
1 1
4 2
1 3
2 4
7 Welcome to Linux shell scripting
```

To get only those lines in file that have appeared only once, the -u option is used:

```
$ sort unique.txt | uniq -u
1

3

Welcome To Linux Shell Scripting
```

Similarly, to get the lines that have been appeared more than once in a file, -d is used:

```
$  sort unique.txt | uniq -d
2

4

Welcome to Linux shell scripting
Welcome to LINUX shell sCripting
```

We can also tell the uniq command to find unique lines based on comparing only the first N character of the line:

```
$ sort unique.txt | uniq -w 10
1
2
3
4
Welcome to Linux shell scripting
Welcome To Linux Shell Scripting
```

- The uniq command does not detect the repeated lines unless they are adjacent.
- To find unique lines, first sort the input using the sort command and then apply the uniq command.

Character-based translation using tr

Another interesting shell command is `tr`. This translates, squeezes, or deletes characters from the standard input. The syntax will be as follows:

```
tr [OPTION]... SET1 [SET2]
```

The options for the `tr` commands are explained in the following table:

Option	Description
`-c`, `-C`	Use complement of SET1
`-d`	This deletes a range of characters specified in SET1.
`-s`	This replaces consecutive multiple occurrences of characters in SET1 with a single occurrence.
`-t`	This truncates SET1 to the length of SET2. Any extra characters in SET1 will be not considered for translation.

SETs are a string of characters that can be specified using the following:

- A character class: `[:alnum:]`, `[:digit:]`, `[:alpha:]` and so on
- A character range: `'a-z'`, `'A-Z'`, and `'0-9'`
- An escape character: `\\`, `\b`, `\r`, `\n`, `\f`, `\v`, and `\t`

To provide an input text from a file and an output to a file, we can use the file redirection operators: < (less than for input) and > (greater than for output).

Deleting input characters

Sometimes, removing a few unnecessary characters from an input text is important. For example, our input text is in the `tr.txt` file:

```
$ cat tr.txt
This is a text file for demonstrating
tr command.
This input file contains digit 2 3 4 and 5
as well.
THIS IS CAPS LINE
this a lowercase line
```

Suppose we want to remove all the caps letters from this file. We can use the `-d` option with SET1 as `'A-Z'`:

```
$ tr -d 'A-Z' < tr.txt
This is a text file for demonstrating
tr command.
This input file contains digit 2 3 4 and 5
as well.


this a lowercase line
```

We see that the output doesn't have any caps letter. We can also removed a new line and space from a file as follows:

```
$ tr -d ' \n' < tr.txt > tr_out1.txt
```

Here, we have redirected the output to `tr_out1.txt`:

```
$ cat tr_out1.txt
```

```
Thisisatextfilefordemonstratingtrcommand.
Thisinputfileconatainsdigit234and5aswell.THISISCAPSLINEthisalowercaseline
```

Squeezing to a single occurrence

The `-s` option is useful when we don't want to delete a character throughout the input text, instead we want to squeeze down to a single occurrence if consecutive multiple occurrences of the given character is there.

One of the use-case where it will prove useful is when we have multiple spaces in between two words that we want to bring down to a single space between any two words/strings in the input text. Consider the `tr1.txt` file as an example:

```
$ cat tr1.txt
India            China              Canada
USA    Japan               Russia
Germany          France             Italy
Australia    Nepal
```

By looking into this file, it's quite clear that texts are not properly aligned. There are multiple spaces between two words. We can squeeze multiple spaces to one space using the `tr` option with `-s`:

```
$ tr -s ' ' < tr1.txt
India China Canada
USA Japan Russia
Germany France Italy
Australia Nepal
```

Inverting a character set to be translated

Command `tr` also provides the `-c` or `-C` options to invert a character set to be translated. This is useful when we know what is not to be translated.

For example, we want to keep only alphanumeric, newline, and white-space in the text string. Everything should be deleted from the input text. Here, it's easy to specify what not to delete rather than what to delete.

For example, consider the `tr2.txt` file whose content is as follows:

```
$ cat tr2.txt
This is an input file.
It conatins special character like ?, ! etc
&^var is an invalid shll variable.
_var1_ is a valid shell variable
```

To delete characters other than alphanumeric, newline, and white-space, we can run the following command:

```
tr -cd '[:alnum:] \n' < tr2.txt
This is an input file
It conatins special character like   etc
var is an invalid shll variable
var1 is a valid shell variable
```

Filtering based on lines—head and tail

To display the content of a file, we will use the `cat` command. The `cat` command displays the whole file content on `stdout`. However, sometimes, we are interested in viewing only a few lines of a file. In this case, using `cat` will be tedious because we will have to scroll down to particular lines that we are interested in.

Shell provides us the `head` and `tail` commands to print only the lines in which we are interested in. The main difference between both the commands is, `head` prints the lines from the beginning of the files, and tail prints the lines from the end of the files.

Printing lines using head

The syntax is as follows:

```
head [OPTION] [FILE ...]
```

By default, `head` prints first 10 lines of each FILE to `stdout`. If no file is mentioned or '-' is specified, the input is taken from `stdin`.

The options available in head can be used to change how much of the content to be printed. The options available are described in the following table:

Option	Description
`-c [-] K`	This prints first K bytes of a file. If -K is used, then you can output all contents except the last K bytes.
`-n [-]K`	This prints first K lines of each file. If -K is used, then you can output all lines except the last n lines.
`-q`	This prevents name of input files from being printed.
`-v`	This always outputs the header having the filename of each file.

Printing the first few lines

Let's see how many files `/usr/lib64/` directory contains -:

```
$ ls /usr/lib64 | wc
3954
```

We see that `/usr/lib64` has 3954 files. Suppose, we don't want all the libraries names, but just the first five library names. We can use a head command for this as follows:

```
$ ls /usr/lib64 | head -n 5
akonadi
alsa-lib
ao
apper
apr-util-1
```

Printing the first few bytes

We use the `-c` option to print the first few bytes of a file, as follows:

```
$ head -c50 /usr/share/dict/linux.words /usr/share/dict/words
==> /usr/share/dict/linux.words <==
1080
10-point
10th
11-point
12-point
```

```
16-point
18-p
==> /usr/share/dict/words <==
1080
10-point
10th
11-point
12-point
16-point
18-p
```

This first prints 50 bytes of the /usr/share/dict/linux.words and /usr/share/dict/words files.

We can eliminate the printing of the header having a filename using -q:

```
$ head -c50 -q  /usr/share/dict/linux.words /usr/share/dict/words
1080
10-point
10th
11-point
12-point
16-point
18-p1080
10-point
10th
11-point
12-point
16-point
18-p
```

For a single file, command head doesn't print name of file in output. To see it, use -v option:

```
$ head -c50 -v  /usr/share/dict/linux.words
==> /usr/share/dict/linux.words <==
1080
10-point
10th
11-point
12-point
16-point
18-p
```

Printing lines using tail

The syntax for `tail` is as follows:

```
tail [OPTION] [FILE ...]
```

By default, `tail` prints the last 10 lines of each `FILE` to `stdout`. If no file is mentioned or '-' is specified, the input is taken from `stdin`.

The options available in `tail` can be used to change how much of the content to be printed. The available options are described in the following table:

Option	Description
`-c [+]K`	This prints the last K byte of each file. If +K is used, then print from Kth byte of each file.
`-n [+]K`	This prints the last K lines of each file. If +K is used, then output from Kth line of each file.
`-f [{name|descriptor}]`	The outputs the appended data as the file grows.
`--retry`	This keeps trying to open a file if it is inaccessible.
`--max-unchanged-stats=N`	With the `-f` name, reopen the file that has not opened. This shows the changed size after N iterations (default 5).
`--pid=PID`	With `-f`, terminate if `PID` dies.
`-q`	Don't output header having filename of each file.
`-F`	This is the same as the `-f` name `--retry` option.
`-s N`	This sleeps for N seconds between iterations. With –pid=PID, check the process at least once in N seconds.
`-v`	This always outputs the header having a filename of each file.

Checking log entries

The `tail` command is frequently used to check the error or message log for the last few run of commands. With each new run, logs are appended at the end of the line.

We will see in following example that kernel log entries are made when a new USB drive is added and when it is removed:

```
$ dmesg | tail -n7    # Log when USB was attached

   [120060.536856] sd 10:0:0:0: Attached scsi generic sg1 type 0
   [120060.540848] sd 10:0:0:0: [sdb] 1976320 512-byte logical blocks:
   (1.01 GB/965 MiB)
   [120060.541989] sd 10:0:0:0: [sdb] Write Protect in off
   [120060.541991] sd 10:0:0:0: [sdb] Mode Sense: 23 00 00 00
```

```
[120060.543125] sd 10:0:0:0: [sdb] Write cache: disabled, read cache:
enabled, doesn't support DPO or FUA
[120060.550464]  sdb: sdb1
[120060.555682] sd 10:0:0:0: [sdb] Attached SCSI removable disk
```

$ dmesg | tail -n7 # USB unmounted

```
[120060.540848] sd 10:0:0:0: [sdb] 1976320 512-byte logical blocks:
(1.01 GB/965 MiB)
[120060.541989] sd 10:0:0:0: [sdb] Write Protect is off
[120060.541991] sd 10:0:0:0: [sdb] Mode Sense: 23 00 00 00
[120060.543125] sd 10:0:0:0: [sdb] Write cache: disabled, read cache:
enabled, doesn't support DPO or FUA
[120060.550464]  sdb: sdb1
[120060.555682] sd 10:0:0:0: [sdb] Attached SCSI removable disk
[120110.466498] sdb: detected capacity change from 1011875840 to 0
```

We saw that when USB was unmounted, a new log entry was
added: `[120110.466498]  sdb:` detected capacity change from `1011875840` to `0`
To check the last 10 yum logs in an RPM-based system, we can do the following:

sudo tail -n4 -v /var/log/yum.log

```
==> /var/log/yum.log-20150320 <==
Mar 19 15:40:19 Updated: libgpg-error-1.17-2.fc21.i686
Mar 19 15:40:19 Updated: libgcrypt-1.6.3-1.fc21.i686
Mar 19 15:40:20 Updated: systemd-libs-216-21.fc21.i686
Mar 19 15:40:21 Updated: krb5-libs-1.12.2-14.fc21.i686
```

To see real-time logs, we can use the `-f` option. For example, the `/var/log/`
`messages` file shows the general system activities. With `tail -f`, appended log
messages in `/var/log/messages` will be printed on `stdout` as well:

$ tail -f /var/log/messages

```
Jun  7 18:21:14 localhost dbus[667]: [system] Rejected send message,
10 matched rules; type="method_return", sender=":1.23" (uid=0 pid=1423
comm="/usr/lib/udisks2/udisksd --no-debug ") interface="(unset)"
member="(unset)" error name="(unset)" requested_reply="0"
destination=":1.355" (uid=1000 pid=25554 comm="kdeinit4: dolphin
[kdeinit] --icon system-fil    ")
Jun  7 18:21:14 localhost systemd-udevd: error: /dev/sdb: No medium
found
Jun  7 18:21:14 localhost systemd-udevd: error: /dev/sdb: No medium
found
Jun  7 18:27:10 localhost kernel: [135288.809319] usb 3-1.2: USB
disconnect, device number 14
Jun  7 18:27:10 localhost kernel: usb 3-1.2: USB disconnect, device
number 14
Jun  7 18:27:10 localhost systemd-udevd: error opening USB device
'descriptors' file
```

The command prompt won't return back. Instead, the output will keep getting updated whenever there is new content in /var/log/messages.

Finding any line in a file

We can use head and tail to find any line of a file.

We will consider the /usr/share/dict/words file as an example.

Now, to find the 10th line of this file, we can do the following:

```
$ head -10 /usr/share/dict/words | tail -n1  # 10th line
20-point


$ head -200000 /usr/share/dict/words | tail -n1  #  200000th line
intracartilaginous
```

The Cut-based selection

We can also select a text from each line of single/multiple files using the cut command. The cut command allows us to select a column based on delimiters. By default, TAB is used as delimiter. We can also select a portion of the text in a line by specifying the characters or range. The syntax is as follows:

```
cut OPTION [FILE ...]
```

The cut command works on the single and multiple files. By default, the output is printed on stdout.

The options for the cut command are explained in the following table:

Option	Description
-b LIST	This selects bytes that are specified in LIST.
-c LIST	This selects characters that are specified in LIST.
-d DELIM	This uses delimiter as DELIM instead of TAB. It also prints lines that don't have a delimiter.
-f LIST	This only selects fields specified in LIST.
--complement	This complements a set of selected bytes, characters, or fields.
-s	Don't print lines that don't have a delimiter.
--output-delimiter=STRING	This uses STRING as the output delimiter. By default, the input delimiter is used.

LIST is made up of a range or many ranges separated by a comma. A range is specified as follows:

Range	Meaning
N	This is the Nth byte, character, or field, counted from 1
N-	This is from the Nth byte, character, or field, to the end of the line
N-M	This is from the Nth to Mth byte (including M and N), character, or field.
-M	This is from the first to Mth (include) byte, character, or field.

Cutting across columns

A lot of Linux command outputs are formatted in such a way that the results have multiple fields and each field is separated by space or tabs. The outputs of each field can be viewed by looking down into a particular field column.

Execute the `ls -l ~` command and observe the following output:

```
$ ls -l ~
```

```
total 20
drwxrwxr-x. 2 sinny sinny 4096 Jun  7 20:06 Desktop
drwxrwxr-x. 2 sinny sinny 4096 Jun  7 20:06 Document
-rw-rw-r--. 1 sinny sinny   68 Jun  7 20:07 example.txt
-rw-rw-r--. 1 sinny sinny    0 Jun  7 20:06 hello.txt
drwxrwxr-x. 2 sinny sinny 4096 Jun  7 20:07 Music
drwxrwxr-x. 2 sinny sinny 4096 Jun  7 20:06 Videos
```

Now, we are interested only in knowing the modification time and filename. To achieve this, we will need the column 6 to 9:

```
$ ls -l ~ | tr -s ' ' |cut -f 6-9 -d ' '
```

```
Jun 7 20:06 Desktop
Jun 7 20:06 Document
Jun 7 20:07 example.txt
Jun 7 20:06 hello.txt
Jun 7 20:07 Music
Jun 7 20:06 Videos
```

By default, TAB is used as a delimiter. Here, there are multiple spaces between any two columns in the `ls -l` output. So, first using `tr -s`, we will squeeze multiple whitespace into single whitespace and then we will cut the column field range 6-9 with a delimiter as whitespace.

Text selection in files

Consider the `cut1.txt` file as an example. The content of the file is as follows:

```
$ cat cut1.txt
```

The output will be:

```
Name      USN      Marks    Department
Foo       AB1      67       CSE
Bar       AB2      98       ECE
Moo       AB3      23       CSE
Bleh      AB4      90       CSE
Worm      AB5      99       Mechanical
Lew       AB6      67       Civil
```

Now, we are interested in knowing the names of the students. We can get this by fetching the first column. Here, each column is separated by *Tab*. So, we will not have to specify the delimiter in our command:

```
$ cut -f1 cut1.txt
Name

Foo

Bar

Moo

Bleh

Worm

Lew
```

Another interesting thing to do is to get unique department names. We can do this by using the following set of commands on the `cut1.txt` file:

```
$ cut -f4 cut1.txt | tail -n +2 | sort -u
Civil

CSE

ECE

Mechanical
```

We can see that there are four unique departments mentioned in the `cut1.txt` file.

Another interesting thing we can do is find out who received the highest marks, as follows:

```
$ cut -f1,3 cut1.txt | tail -n +2 | sort -k2 -nr | head -n1
Worm      99
```

To find out who scored the highest mark, we first select the first and third column from the `cut1.txt` file. Then, we exclude the first line using `tail -n +2`, which tells us what this file is about, because we do not need this. After that, we do numerical sorting of the second column in reverse order, which contains the marks of all the students. Now, we know that the first column contains the details of those who scored the highest marks.

Knowing the speed of your system processor is interesting in order to know the various details of your system. Among all, one of them knows the speed of your processor. The first thing to know is that all processor details are available in the `/proc/cpuinfo` file. You can open this file and see what all details are available. For example, we know that the processor's speed is mentioned in the `"model name"` field.

The following shell script will show the speed of the processor:

```
#!/bin/bash
#Filename: process_speed.sh
#Description: Demonstrating how to find processor speed ofrunning
system

grep -R "model name" /proc/cpuinfo | sort -u > /tmp/tmp1.txt
tr -d ' ' </tmp/tmp1.txt > /tmp/tmp2.txt
cut -d '@' -f2 /tmp/tmp2.txt
```

Running this script will output the processor speed of your system:

```
$ sh processor_speed.sh
2.80GHz
```

We can also do without using temporary files:

```
$ grep -R "model name" /proc/cpuinfo | sort -u | cut -d '@' -f2
2.80GHz
```

Summary

After reading this chapter, you should know how to provide an input to commands and print or save its result. You should also be familiar with redirecting an output and input from one command to another. Now, you can easily search, replace strings or pattern in a file, and filter out data based on needs.

From this chapter, we now have a good control on transforming/filtering text data. In next chapter, we will learn how to write more powerful and useful shell scripts by learning loops, conditions, switch, and the most important function in shell. We will also know how important it is to know the exit status of a command. In the next chapter, we will also see more advanced examples of commands that we have learned in this chapter.

3
Effective Script Writing

To write an effective script in shell, it is very important to know about the different utilities that shell provides. Similar to other programming languages, shell programming also requires a way to specify skipping or running certain commands under certain conditions. To perform a certain task on the list of elements, looping constructs are needed in shell as well.

In this chapter, we will cover topics such as `if`, `else`, `case`, and `select` that can be used to run a certain block of commands according to the condition. We will see the `for`, `while`, and `until` constructs, which are used to loop over a certain block of commands in a script. We will see how the exit code, after the execution of a command or script, plays an important role in knowing whether a command was executed successfully or not. We will also see how a function can be defined in shell, which will allow us to write modular and reusable code from now on.

This chapter will cover the following topics in detail:

- Exiting from scripts and exit codes
- Testing expressions with a test
- Using conditional statements with `if` and `else`
- Indexed arrays and associative arrays
- Looping around with `for`
- The `select`, `while`, and `until` loops
- Switching to your choice
- Using functions and positional parameters
- Passing `stdout` as a parameter using `xargs`
- Aliases
- `pushd` and `popd`

Exiting from scripts and exit codes

We are now well familiar with shell script files, commands, and running them in bash to get the desired output. Until now, whatever shell script examples we have seen, they run line by line until the end of the file. While writing real-world shell scripts, it may not always be the case. We may need to exit a script in between, for example, when some error occurs, doesn't satisfy a certain condition, and so on. To exit from the script, the exit shell builtin is used with an optional return value. The return value tells the exit code, which is also known as return status or exit status.

Exit codes

Every command returns an exit code when it gets executed. Exit code is one of the ways to know whether a command is executed successfully or if some error has occurred. As per the **POSIX (Portable Operating System Interface)** standard convention, a command or program with successful execution returns 0, and 1 or a higher value for failed execution.

In bash, to see the exit status of the last command executed, we can use "$?".

The following example shows the exit code of the successful command execution:

```
$ ls /home   # viewing Content of directory /home
foo
```

Now, to see the exit code of the last executed command, that is, ls /home, we will run the following command:

```
$ echo $?
0
```

We see that the exit status of the ls command execution is 0, which means it has executed successfully.

Another example showing the exit code of the unsuccessful command execution is as follows:

```
$  ls /root/
ls: cannot open directory /root/: Permission denied
```

We see that the ls command execution was unsuccessful with the Permission denied error. To see the exit status, run the following command:

```
$ echo $?
2
```

The exit status code is 2, which is higher than 0, representing unsuccessful execution.

Exit codes with a special meaning

In different situations, a different exit code is returned by a script or command. Knowing the meaning of the exit code is useful while debugging a script or command. The following table explains which exit code is conventionally returned in different conditions of command or script execution:

Exit code	Description
0	Successful execution
1	General error
2	Error when using shell builtin commands
126	Permission issues while executing a command; we can't invoke the requested command
127	Could not invoke requested command
128	Specifying invalid argument to exit in script. Only value from 0 to 255 is valid exit code
128+n	Fatal error with the signal 'n'
130	Terminating script using Ctl + C
255*	Out of the range exit code

Exit codes 0, 1, 126-165, and 255 are reserved and we should use other than these numbers when we return the exit code in script files.

The following examples show the different exit codes returned by commands:

- **Exit code 0**: The following is the successful execution of the echo command:

```
$ echo "Successful Exit code check"
Successful Exit code check
$ echo $?
0
```

- **Exit code 1**: Copying files from /root have no permissions as shown:

```
$  cp -r /root/ .
cp: cannot access '/root/': Permission denied
$ echo $?
1
```

- **Exit code 2**: Use read shell builtin with an invalid parameter as follows:

```
$ echo ;;
bash: syntax error near unexpected token ';;'
$ echo $?
2
```

- **Exit code 126**: Run a `/usr/bin` directory as a command that is actually not a command:

```
$ /usr/bin
bash: /usr/bin: Is a directory
$ echo $?
126
```

- **Exit code 127**: Run a command named `foo` that is not actually present in the system:

```
$ foo
bash: foo: command not found
$ echo $?
127
```

- **Exit code 128+n**: Terminate a script by pressing *Ctrl + C*:

```
$ read

^C
$ echo $?
130
```

Here, *Ctrl + C* sends the SIGQUIT signal whose value is 2. So, the exit code is 130 (128 + 2).

Script with exit codes

We can also exit shell builtin along with an exit code to know whether a script ran successfully or it encountered any error. Different error codes can be used to know the actual reason of an error while debugging your own script.

When we don't provide any exit code in a script, the exit code of the script is determined by the last executed command:

```
#!/bin/bash

# Filename: without_exit_code.sh
# Description: Exit code of script when no exit code is mentioned in script


var="Without exit code in script"
echo $var

cd /root
```

The preceding script doesn't specify any exit code; running this script will give the following output:

```
$ sh without_exit_code.sh
Without exit code in script
without_exit_code.sh: line 8: cd: /root: Permission denied
$ echo $?  # checking exit code of script
1
```

The exit code of this script is 1 because we didn't specify any exit code and the last executed command was cd /root, which failed due to a permission issue.

Taking the next example that returns the exit code 0, irrespective of any error that occurs — that is, script ran successfully:

```
#!/bin/bash

# Filename: with_exit_code.sh
# Description: Exit code of script when exit code is mentioned in scr#
ipt


var="Without exit code in script"
echo $var

cd /root

exit 0
```

Running this script will give the following result:

```
$ sh with_exit_code.sh
Without exit code in script
with_exit_code.sh: line 8: cd: /root: Permission denied
echo $?
0
```

Now, the script file returns the exit code as 0. We now know what a difference adding an exit code in script can make.

Another example with the exit status code is as follows:

```
#!/bin/bash
# Filename: exit_code.sh
# Description: Exit code of script


cmd_foo # running command not installed in system
echo $?

cd /root # Permission problem
echo $?

echo "Hello World!" # Successful echo print
echo $?

exit 200 # Returning script's exit code as 200
```

The output after running this script is as follows:

```
$ sh exit_status.sh
exit_code.sh: line 5: cmd_foo: command not found
127
exit_code.sh: line 8: cd: /root: Permission denied
1
Hello World!
0
$ echo $?   # Exit code of script
200
```

If no exit code is specified in a script, the exit code will be the exit status of the last command ran in the script.

Testing expressions with a test

The shell builtin command `test` can be used to check file types and compare expressions value. The syntax is `test EXPRESSION` or the `test` command is also equivalent to **[EXPRESSION]**.

It returns the exit code 1 (`false`) if the EXPRESSION result is 0, and 0 (`true`) for a non-zero EXPRESSION result.

If no EXPRESSION is provided, the exit status is set to 1 (false).

File checks

Different kinds of checks can be done on the file using the `test` command; for example, file existence test, directory test, regular file check, symbolic link check, and so on.

The options available to do various checks on a file are explained in the following table:

Option	Description
-e	fileChecks whether the file exists
-f file	The file is a regular fil
-d file	The file exists and is a directory
-h, -L file	The file is a symbolic link
-b file	The file is block special
-c file	The file is character special
-S file	The file is a socket
-p file	The file is a named pipe
-k file	Sticky bit of the file is set
-g file	set-group-ID (sgid) bit of the file is set
-u file	set-user-id (suid) bit of the file is set
-r file	Read permission on the file exists
-w file	Write permission on the file exists
-x file	Execute permission on the file exists
-t fd	File descriptor fd is open on terminal
file1 -ef file2	file1 is hard link to file2
file1 -nt file2	file1 is more recent compared to file2
file1 -ot file2	The modification time of file1 is older than file2

Shell script performs different checks on the files as follows:

```bash
#!/bin/bash
# Filename: file_checks.sh
# Description: Performing different check on and between files

# Checking existence of /tmp/file1
echo -n "Does File /tmp/file1 exist? "
test -e /tmp/file1
echo $?

# Create /tmp/file1
touch /tmp/file1 /tmp/file2
echo -n "Does file /tmp/file1 exist now? "
test -e /tmp/file1
echo $?

# Check whether /tmp is a directory or not
echo -n "Is /tmp a directory? "
test -d /tmp
echo $?

# Checking if sticky bit set on /tmp"
echo -n "Is sticky bit set on /tmp ? "
test -k /tmp
echo $?

# Checking if /tmp has execute permission
echo -n "Does /tmp/ has execute permission ? "
test -x /tmp
echo $?

# Creating another file /tmp/file2
touch /tmp/file2

# Check modification time of /tmp/file1 and /tmp/file2
echo -n "Does /tmp/file1 modified more recently than /tmp/file2 ? "
test /tmp/file1 -nt /tmp/file2
echo $?
```

The output of running this script is as follows:

```
Does File /tmp/file1 exist? 1
Does file /tmp/file1 exist now? 0
Is /tmp a directory? 0
Is sticky bit set on /tmp ? 0
Does /tmp/ has execute permission? 0
Does /tmp/file1 modified more recently than /tmp/file2 ? 1
```

In our output, 0 and 1 are the exist status after running a test command on files. The output 1 means the test failed and 0 means the test was successfully passed.

Arithmetic checks

We can also perform arithmetic checks between integer numbers. Comparison possible on integers is explained to following table:

Comparison	Description
INTEGER1 -eq INTEGER2	INTEGER1 is equal to INTEGER2
INTEGER1 -ne INTEGER2	INTEGER1 is not equal to INTEGER2
INTEGER1 -gt INTEGER2	INTEGER1 is greater than INTEGER2
INTEGER1 -ge INTEGER2	INTEGER1 is greater than or equal to INTEGER2
INTEGER1 -lt INTEGER2	INTEGER1 is lesser than INTEGER2
INTEGER1 -le INTEGER2	INTEGER1 is lesser than or equal to INTEGER2

Shell script shows various arithmetic checks between two integers as follows:

```
#!/bin/bash
# Filename: integer_checks.sh
# Description: Performing different arithmetic checks between integers

a=12 b=24 c=78 d=24
echo "a = $a , b = $b , c = $c , d = $d"

echo -n "Is a greater than b ? "
test $a -gt $b
echo $?

echo -n "Is b equal to d ? "
test $b -eq $d
echo $?
```

```
echo -n "Is c not equal to d ? "
test $c -ne $d
echo $?
```

The output of running this script is as follows:

```
a = 12 , b = 24 , c = 78 , d = 24
Is a greater than b ? 1
Is b equal to d ? 0
Is c not equal to d ? 0
```

Also, here the test returns the exit status after running a comparison test between integers, and returns 0 (true) on success and 1 (false) if the test fails.

String checks

A command test also allows you to perform checks on and between strings. The possible checks are described in the following table:

Comparison	Description
-z STRING	The length of the string is zero
-n STRING	The length of the string is non-zero
STRING1 = STRING2	STRING1 and STRING2 are equal
SRING1 != STRING2	STRING1 and STRING2 are not equal

Shell script shows various string checks on and between strings as follows:

```
#!/bin/bash
# Filename: string_checks.sh
# Description: Performing checks on and between strings

str1="Hello" str2="Hell" str3="" str4="Hello"
echo "str1 = $str1 , str2 = $str2 , str3 = $str3 , str4 = $str4"

echo -n "Is str3 empty ? "
test -z $str3
echo $?

echo -n "Is str2 not empty? "
test -n $str2
echo $?
```

```
echo -n "Are str1 and str4 equal? "
test $str1 = $str4
echo $?

echo -n "Are str1 and str2 different? "
test $str1 != $str2
echo $?
```

The output of running this script is as follows:

```
str1 = Hello , str2 = Hell , str3 =  , str4 = Hello
Is str3 empty ? 0
Is str2 not empty? 0
Are str1 and str4 equal? 0
Are str1 and str2 different? 0
```

Here, the test returns 0 exit status if the string checks are true, else returns 1.

Expression checks

The test command also allows you to perform checks on and between expressions. An expression itself can contain multiple expressions to evaluate as well. The possible checks done are explained in the following table:

Comparison	Description
(EXPRESSION)	This EXPRESSION is true
! EXPRESSION	This EXPRESSION is false
EXPRESSION1 -a EXPRESSION2	Both the expressions are true (the AND operation)
EXPRESSION1 -o EXPRESSION2	Either one of the expressions is true (the OR operation)

Shell script shows various string checks on and between strings as follows:

```
#!/bin/bash
# Filename: expression_checks.sh
# Description: Performing checks on and between expressions

a=5 b=56
str1="Hello" str2="Hello"

echo "a = $a , b = $b , str1 = $str1 , str2 = $str2"
```

```
echo -n "Is a and b are not equal, and str1 and str2 are equal? "
test ! $a -eq $b -a  $str1 = $str2
echo $?

echo -n "Is a and b are equal, and str1 and str2 are equal? "
test $a -eq $b -a  $str1 = $str2
echo $?

echo -n "Does /tmp is a sirectory and execute permission exists? "
test -d /tmp -a  -x /tmp
echo $?

echo -n "Is /tmp file is a block file or write permission exists? "
test -b /tmp -o -w /tmp
echo $?
```

The output of running this script is as follows:

```
a = 5 , b = 56 , str1 = Hello , str2 = Hello
Is a and b are not equal, and str1 and str2 are equal? 0
Is a and b are equal, and str1 and str2 are equal? 1
Does /tmp is a sirectory and execute permission exists? 0
Is /tmp file is a block file or write permission exists? 0
```

Similar to other checks with the test command, the 0 exit code means the expression evaluated is true and 1 means false evaluation.

Using conditional statements with if and else

Shell provides if and else to run conditional statements depending upon whether the evaluation is true or false. It is useful if we want to perform certain tasks only if a certain condition is true.

The test condition to if can be given using a test condition or [condition]. We have already learned multiple use cases and examples of testing an expression in the previous section, *Testing expressions with a test*.

Simple if and else

The syntax of the `if` condition is as follows:

```
if [ conditional_expression ]
then
  statements
fi
```

If `conditional_expression` is `true` — that is, the exit status is `0` — then the statements inside it get executed. If not, then it will be just be ignored and the next line after `fi` will be executed.

The syntax of `if` and `else` is as follows:

```
if [ conditional_expression ]
then
  statements
else
  statements
fi
```

Sometimes, when a condition is not true, we might want to execute some statements. In such cases, use `if` and `else`. Here, if `conditional_statement` is true, statements within if get executed. Otherwise, statements within else will be executed.

The following shell script prints the message if a file exists:

```
#!/bin/bash
# Filename: file_exist.sh
# Description: Print message if file exists

if [ -e /usr/bin/ls ]
then
        echo "File /usr/bin/ls exists"
fi
```

The output after running the script is as follows:

```
File /usr/bin/ls exists
```

Another example shows the greater one among two integers as follows:

```
#!/bin/bash
# Filename: greater_integer.sh
# Description: Determining greater among two integers

echo "Enter two integers a and b"
read a b          # Reading input from stdin
echo "a = $a , b = $b"
# Finding greater integer
if test $a -gt $b
then
        echo "a is greater than b"
else
        echo "b is greater than a"
fi
```

The following is the output after running the script:

```
$ sh greater_integer.sh
Enter two integers a and b
56 8
a = 56 , b = 8
a is greater than b
```

The if, elif, and else statements

In some cases, more than two choices exist, of which only one needs to be executed. The elif allows you to use another if condition instead of using else if a condition is not true. The syntax is as follows:

```
if [ conditional_expression1 ]
then
   statements
elif [ conditional_expression2 ]
then
   statements
elif [ conditional_expression3 ]
then
   statements
   # More elif conditions
else
   statements
```

The following shell script will make the `elif` usage more clear. This script asks a user to input a valid file or directory name with the absolute path. On a valid regular file or directory, it displays the following content:

```
#!/bin/bash
# Filename: elif_usage.sh
# Description: Display content if user input is a regular file or a
directoy

echo "Enter a valid file or directory path"
read path
echo "Entered path is $path"

if [ -f $path ]
then
    echo "File is a regular file and its content is:"
    cat $path
elif [ -d $path ]
then
    echo "File is a directory and its content is:"
    ls $path
else
    echo "Not a valid regular file or directory"
fi
```

The output after running the script is as follows:

```
Enter a valid file or directory path
/home/
Entered path is /home/
File is a directory and its content is:
lost+found  sinny
```

Nested if

In many cases, multiple `if` conditions are required because the execution of a condition depends upon the result of another condition. The syntax will be as follows:

```
if [ conditional_expression1 ]
then
  if [ conditional_expression2 ]
  then
```

```
       statements
       if [conditional_expression3 ]
       then
          statements
       fi
   fi
fi
```

The following script example explains the nested if in more detail. In this script, we will see how to find the greatest one of the three integer values:

```
#!/bin/bash
# Filename: nested_if.sh
# Description: Finding greatest integer among 3 by making use of
nested if

echo "Enter three integer value"
read a b c
echo "a = $a , b = $b, c = $c"

if [ $a -gt $b ]
then
    if [ $a -gt $c ]
    then
        echo "a is the greatest integer"
    else
       echo "c is the greatest integer"
    fi
else
   if [ $b -gt $c ]
   then
      echo "b is the greatest integer"
   else
      echo "c is the greatest integer"
   fi
fi
```

The output after running the script will be as follows:

```
Enter three integer value
78 110 7
a = 78 , b = 110, c = 7
b is the greatest integer
```

Indexed arrays and associative arrays

Bash provides a feature to declare a list (or array) of variables in a one-dimensional array that can be an indexed array or associative array. The size of an array can be 0 or more.

Indexed arrays

An indexed array contains variables that may or may not have been initialized continuously. Indices of an indexed array start from 0. This means that the first element of an array will start at an index 0.

Array declaration and value assignment

An indexed array can be declared by just initializing any index as follows:

```
array_name[index]=value
```

Here, an index can be any positive integer or an expression must be evaluated to a positive integer.

Another way of declaring is by using the `declare` shell built in as follows:

```
declare -a array_name
```

We can also initialize an array with values during a declaration. Values are enclosed within parentheses and each value is separated with a blank space as follows:

```
declare -a array_name=(value1 value2 value3 …)
```

Operations on arrays

Initializing and declaring values to a variable is not sufficient. The actual usage of an array is when we perform different operations on it to get the desired result.

The following operations can be done on an indexed array:

- Accessing an array element by an index: An element of an array can be accessed by referring to its index value:

  ```
  echo ${array_name[index]}
  ```

- Printing the array's contents: The contents of an array can be printed if an index of an array is given as @ or *:

  ```
  echo ${array_name[*]}
  echo ${array_name[@]}
  ```

- Obtaining the length of an array: The length of an array can be obtained using $# with the array variable:

```
echo ${#array_name[@]}
echo ${#array_name[*]}
```

- Obtaining the length of an array element: The length of an array element can be obtained using $# on nth index:

```
echo ${#array_name[n]}
```

- Deleting an element or an entire array: An element can be removed from an array using the unset keyword:

```
unset array_name[index]   # Removes value at index

unset array_name  # Deletes entire array
```

The following shell script demonstrates the different operations on an indexed array:

```
#!/bin/bash
# Filename: indexed_array.sh
# Description: Demonstrating different operations on indexed array

#Declaring an array conutries and intializing it
declare -a countries=(India Japan Indonesia 'Sri Lanka' USA Canada)

# Printing Length and elements of countries array
echo "Length of array countries = ${#countries[@]}"
echo ${countries[@]}

# Deleting 2nd element of array
unset countries[1]
echo "Updated length and content of countries array"
echo "Length = ${#countries[@]}"
echo ${countries[@]}

# Adding two more countries to array
countries=("${countries[@]}" "Indonesia" "England")
echo "Updated length and content of countries array"
echo "Length = ${#countries[@]}"
echo ${countries[@]}
```

The output after executing this script is as follows:

```
Length of array countries = 6
India Japan Indonesia Sri Lanka USA Canada
Updated length and content of countries array
Length = 5
India Indonesia Sri Lanka USA Canada
Updated length and content of countries array
Length = 7
India Indonesia Sri Lanka USA Canada Indonesia England
```

The associative array

The associative array contains a list of elements in which each element has a key-value pair. The elements of an associative array are not referred by using an integer value 0 to N. It is referred by providing a key name that contains a corresponding value. Each key name should be unique.

The declaration and value assignment

The declaration of an associative array is done by using the -A option with the `declare` shell builtin as follows:

```
declare -A array_name
```

An associate array uses a key instead of an index within a square bracket in order to initialize a value as follows:

```
array_name[key]=value
```

Multiple values can be initialized in the following way:

```
array_name=([key1]=value1 [key2]=value2 ...)
```

Operations on arrays

A few operations on an associative array can be done similar to how an indexed array does, such as printing the length and content of an array. The operations are as follows:

- Accessing an array element by the key name; to access an element of an associative array, use a unique key as follows:

```
echo ${array_name[key]}
```

- Printing associative array content: The following syntax is used to print an associative array:

```
echo ${array_name[*]}
echo ${array_name[@]}
Obtaining the length of an array:
echo ${#array_name[@]}
echo ${#array_name[*]}
```

- Getting the value and length of a given key:

```
echo ${array_name[k]}   # Value of key k
echo ${#array_name[k]}   # Length of value of key k
```

- Adding a new element; to add a new element in an associative array, use the += operator as follows:

```
array_name+=([key]=value)
```

- Deleting an element of an associative array with the k key as follows:

```
unset array_name[k]
```

- Deleting an associative array array_name as follows:

```
unset array_name
```

The following shell script demonstrates the different operations on an associative array:

```
#!/bin/bash
# Filename: associative_array.sh
# Description: Demonstrating different operations on associative array

# Declaring a new associative array
declare -A student

# Assigning different fields in student array
student=([name]=Foo [usn]=2D [subject]=maths [marks]=67)

# Printing length and content of array student
echo "Length of student array = ${#student[@]}"
echo ${student[@]}

# deleting element with key marks
unset student[marks]
```

```
echo "Updated array content:"
echo ${student[@]}

# Adding department in student array
student+=([department]=Electronics)
echo "Updated array content:"
echo ${student[@]}
```

The output after executing this script is as follows:

```
Length of student array = 4
Foo 67 maths 2D
Updated array content:
Foo maths 2D
Updated array content:
Foo maths Electronics 2D
```

Looping around with for

The `for` loop can be used to iterate over the items in a list or till the condition is true.

The syntax of using the `for` loop in bash is as follows:

```
for item in [list]
do
    #Tasks
done
```

Another way of writing the `for` loop is the way C does, as follows:

```
for (( expr1; expr2; expr3 ))
  # Tasks
done
```

Here, `expr1` is initialization, `expr2` is condition, and `expr3` is increment.

Simple iteration

The following shell script explains how we can use the `for` loop to print the values of a list:

```
#!/bin/bash
# Filename: for_loop.sh
# Description: Basic for loop in bash
```

```
declare -a names=(Foo Bar Tom Jerry)
echo "Content of names array is:"
for name in ${names[@]}
do
    echo -n "$name "
done
echo
```

The output of the script is as follows:

```
Content of names array is:
Foo Bar Tom Jerry
```

Iterating over a command output

We know that a lot of commands give multiline output such as `ls`, `cat`, `grep`, and so on. In many cases, it makes sense to loop over each line of output and do further processing on them.

The following example loops over the content of '/' and prints directories:

```
#!/bin/bash
# Filename: finding_directories.sh
# Description: Print which all files in / are directories

echo "Directories in / :"
for file in 'ls /'
do
  if [ -d "/"$file ]
  then
      echo -n  "/$file "
  fi
done
echo
```

The output after running this script is as follows:

```
Directories in / :
/bin /boot /dev /etc /home /lib /lib64 /lost+found /media /mnt /opt /
proc /root /run /sbin /srv /sys /tmp /usr /var
```

Specifying a range to the for loop

We can also specify a range of integers in the `for` loop with an optional increment value for it:

```bash
#!/bin/bash
# Filename: range_in_for.sh
# Description: Specifying range of numbers to for loop

echo "Numbers between 5 to 10 -"
for num in {5..10}
do
   echo -n "$num "
done

echo
echo "Odd numbers between 1 to 10 -"
for num in {1..10..2}
do
   echo -n "$num "
done
echo
```

The output after running this script is as follows:

```
Numbers between 5 to 10 -
5 6 7 8 9 10
Odd numbers between 1 to 10 -
1 3 5 7 9
```

Small and sweet for loop

In some cases, we don't want to write a script and then execute it; rather, we prefer to do a job in shell itself. In such cases, it is very useful and handy to write the complete for loop in one line, rather than making it multiline.

For example, printing the multiples of 3 between 3 to 20 numbers can be done with the following code:

```bash
$ for num in {3..20..3}; do echo -n "$num " ; done
   3 6 9 12 15 18
```

The select, while, and until loops

The select, while and until loops are also used to loop and iterate over each item in a list or till the condition is true with slight variations in syntax.

Loop using select

The select loop helps in creating a numbered menu in an easy format from which a user can select one or more options.

The syntax of the select loop is as follows:

```
select var in list
do
    # Tasks to perform
done
```

The list can be pre-generated or specified while using the select loop in the form [item1 item2 item3 …].

For example, consider a simple menu listing the contents of '/' and asking a user to enter an option for which you want to know whether it is a directory or not:

```
#!/bin/bash
# Filename: select.sh
# Description: Giving user choice using select to choose

select file in 'ls /'
do
   if [ -d "/"$file ]
   then
     echo "$file is a directory"
   else
     echo "$file is not a directory"
  fi
done
```

The following is the screenshot of the output after running the script:

```
 1) bin                                12) mnt
 2) boot                               13) opt
 3) dev                                14) proc
 4) etc                                15) root
 5) home                               16) run
 6) kdeinit5__0                        17) sbin
 7) klauncherT14835.1.slave-socket     18) srv
 8) lib                                19) sys
 9) lib64                              20) tmp
10) lost+found                         21) usr
11) media                              22) var
#? 2
boot is a directory
#? 5
home is a directory
#? 7
klauncherT14835.1.slave-socket is not a siretcory
```

To exit from the script, press *Ctrl + C*.

The while loop

The while loop allows you to do repetitive tasks until the condition is true. The syntax is very similar to what we have in the C and C++ programming language, which is as follows:

```
while [ condition ]
do
    # Task to perform
done
```

For example, read the name of the application and display pids of all the running instances of that application, as follows:

```
#!/bin/bash
# Filename: while_loop.sh
# Description: Using while loop to read user input

echo "Enter application name"
while read line
do
   echo -n "Running PID of application $line :"
   pidof $line
done
```

The output after running this script is as follows:

```
Enter application name
firefox
Running PID of application firefox : 1771
bash
Running PID of application bash : 9876 9646 5333 4388 3970 2090 2079
2012 1683 1336
ls
Running PID of application ls:
systemd
Running PID of application systemd : 1330 1026 1
```

To exit from the script, press *Ctrl + C.*

The until loop

The until loop is very similar to the while loop, but the only difference is that it executes code block until the condition executes to false. The syntax of until is as follows:

```
until condition
do
      # Task to be executed
  done
```

For example, consider that we are interested in knowing pid of an application whenever any instance of it is running. For this, we can use until and check pidof of an application at a certain interval using sleep. When we find pid, we can exit from the until loop and print pid of the running instance of the application.

The following shell script demonstrates the same:

```
#!/bin/bash
# Filename: until_loop.sh
# Description: Using until loop to read user input

echo "Enter application name"
read app
until  pidof $app
do
  sleep 5
done
echo "$app is running now with pid `pidof $app`
```

The output after executing this script is as follows:

```
Enter application name
firefox
1867
firefox is running now with pid 1867
```

Switch to my choice

Switch is used to jump and run a certain case as per the result of the condition or expression is evaluated. It acts as an alternative to using multiple **if** in bash and keeps bash script much clear and readable.

The syntax of `switch` is as follows:

```
case $variable in
  pattern1)
  # Tasks to be executed
  ;;
  pattern2)
  # Tasks to be executed
  ;;
  ...
  pattern n)
  # Tasks to be executed
  ;;
  *)
esac
```

In syntax, `$variable` is the expression or value that needs to be matched among the list of choices provided.

In each choice, a pattern or a combination of patterns can be specified. The `;;` tells bash that end of given choice block. The `esac` keyword specify end of case block.

The following is an example to count the number of files and directories in a given path:

```
#!/bin/bash
# Filename: switch_case.sh
# Description: Using case to find count of directories and files in a
# path
```

```
echo "Enter target path"
read path
files_count=0
dirs_count=0

for file in 'ls -l $path | cut -d ' ' -f1'
do
  case "$file" in

        d*)
        dirs_count='expr $dirs_count + 1 '
        ;;
        -*)
        files_count='expr $files_count + 1'
        ;;
        *)
  esac
done

echo "Directories count = $dirs_count"
echo "Regular file count = $files_count"
```

The output after running this script is as follows:

```
Enter target path
/usr/lib64
Directories count = 134
Regular file count = 1563
```

In this example, we first read an input path from a user using the read shell builtin. Then, we initialize the counter variable of files and directories count to 0. Furthermore, we use ls -l $path | cut -d ' ' -f1 to get a long list of file attributes of the path content and then retrieve its first column. We know that the first character of the first column of ls -l tells the type of the file. If it is d, then it is a directory, and - represents a regular file. The dirs_count or files_count variables get incremented accordingly.

Passing stdout as a parameter using xargs

The `xargs` command is used to build and execute a command line from a standard input. Commands such as `cp`, `echo`, `rm`, `wc`, and so on, don't take input from a standard input or redirected output from another command. In such commands, we can use `xargs` to provide an input as an output of another command. The syntax is as follows:

```
xargs [option]
```

Some of options are explained in the following table:

Option	Description
-a file	This reads items from a file instead of stdin
-0, --null	Inputs are null-terminated instead of whitespace
-t, --verbose	Prints a command line on a standard output before executing
--show-limits	This displays the limit on the length of the command line imposed by OS
-P max-procs	Runs upto the max-procs processes one at a time
-n max-args	This at most uses the max-args argument per command line

Basic operations with xargs

The `xargs` command can be used without any option. It allows you to enter an input from stdin, and when `ctrl + d` is called, it prints whatever was typed:

```
$ xargs
Linux shell
scripting
ctrl + d
Linux shell scripting
```

The `--show-limits` option can be used to know the limit of the command line length:

```
$ xargs --show-limits
Your environment variables take up 4017 bytes
POSIX upper limit on argument length (this system): 2091087
POSIX smallest allowable upper limit on argument length (all systems):
4096
Maximum length of command we could actually use: 2087070
Size of command buffer we are actually using: 131072
```

Using xargs to find a file with the maximum size

The following shell script will explain how `xargs` can be used to get a file with the maximum size in a given directory recursively:

```
#!/bin/bash
# Filename: max_file_size.sh
# Description: File with maximum size in a directory recursively

echo "Enter path of directory"
read path
echo "File with maximum size:"

find $path -type f | xargs du -h | sort -h | tail -1
```

The output after running this script is as follows:

```
Enter path of directory
/usr/bin
File with maximum size:
12M     /usr/bin/doxygen
```

In this example, we are using `xargs` to pass each regular file obtained from the `find` command for size calculation. Furthermore, the output of `du` is redirected to the `sort` command for a human-numeric sort and then we can print the last line or sort to get the file with a maximum size.

Archiving files with a given pattern

Another useful example of using xargs is to archive all the files that we are interested in, and these files can be kept as back files.

The following shell script finds all the shell script in a specified directory and creates tar of it for further reference:

```
#!/bin/bash
# Filename: tar_creation.sh
# Description: Create tar of all shell scripts in a directory

echo "Specify directory path"
read path

find $path -name "*.sh" | xargs tar cvf scripts.tar
```

The output after running the script is as follows:

```
Specify directory path
/usr/lib64
/usr/lib64/nspluginwrapper/npviewer.sh
/usr/lib64/xml2Conf.sh
/usr/lib64/firefox/run-mozilla.sh
/usr/lib64/libreoffice/ure/bin/startup.sh
```

In this example, all the files with an extension .sh are searched and passed as parameters to the tar command to create an archive. The file scripts.tar is created in the directory from where the scripts are being called.

Using functions and positional parameters

Similar to other programming languages, function is a way to write a set of actions once and use it multiple times. It makes the code modular and reusable.

The syntax of writing a function is as follows:

```
function function_name
  {
   # Common set of action to be done
  }
```

Here, `function` is a keyword to specify a function and `function_name` is the name of the function; we can also define a function in the following ways:

```
function_name()
{
  # Common set of action to be done
}
```

The actions written within curly braces are executed whenever a particular function is invoked.

Calling a function in bash

Consider the following shell script that defines the `my_func()` function:

```
#!/bin/bash
# Filename: function_call.sh
# Description: Shows how function is defined and called in bash

# Defining my_func function
my_func()
{
   echo "Function my_func is called"
   return 3
}

my_func # Calling my_func function
return_value=$?
echo "Return value of function = $return_value"
```

To call `my_func()` in shell script, we just have to write a function's name:

```
my_func
```

The `my_func` function has a return value as 3. The return value of a function is the exit status of a function. In the preceding example, the exit status of the `my_func` function is assigned to the `return_value` variable.

The result of running the preceding script is as follows:

```
Function my_func is called
Return value of function = 3
```

The return value of a function is what the return shell builtin is specified in its argument. If no return is used, then the exit code of the last command is executed in the function. In this example, the exit code will be the exit code of the echo command.

Passing parameters to functions

An argument to a function can be provided by specifying the first name of the function followed by space-separated arguments. A function in shell doesn't use parameters by its name but by positions; we can also say that the shell function takes positional parameters. Positional parameters are accessed by the variable names $1, $2, $3, $n, and so on, inside a function.

The length of arguments can be obtained using $#, a list of arguments passed can be fetched together using $@ or $*.

The following shell script explains how parameters are passed to the function in bash:

```
#!/bin/bash
# Filename: func_param.sh
# Description: How parameters to function is passed and accessed in
bash

upper_case()
{
    if [ $# -eq 1 ]
    then
        echo $1 | tr '[a-z]' '[A-Z]'
    fi
}

upper_case hello
upper_case "Linux shell scripting"
```

The output of the preceding script is as follows:

```
HELLO
LINUX SHELL SCRIPTING
```

In the preceding shell script example, we called the upper_case() method twice with the hello and Linux shell scripting parameters. Both of them get converted to uppercase. In a similar way, other functions can be written to avoid writing repetitive work again and again.

Alias

Alias in shell refers to giving another name to a command or group of commands. It is very useful when a name of a command is long. With the help of alias, we can avoid typing a bigger name and invoke a command by a name as per your convenience.

To create an alias, alias shell builtin command is used. The syntax is as follows:

```
alias alias_name="Commands to be aliased"
```

Creating alias

To print a disk space in a human-readable format, we use the df command with the -h option. By making alias of df -h to df, we can avoid typing again and again df -h.

The output of the df command before aliasing it to df -h is shown in the following screenshot:

```
$ df
```

```
Filesystem      1K-blocks      Used Available Use% Mounted on
devtmpfs          3916488         0   3916488   0% /dev
tmpfs             3926460       328   3926132   1% /dev/shm
tmpfs             3926460      1144   3925316   1% /run
tmpfs             3926460         0   3926460   0% /sys/fs/cgroup
/dev/sda1        39573920  14156704  23383912  38% /
tmpfs             3926460       292   3926168   1% /tmp
/dev/dm-0       206287288  88348884 107436264  46% /home
tmpfs              785296         0    785296   0% /run/user/990
tmpfs              785296        36    785260   1% /run/user/1000
```

Now, to create alias for df -h to df, we will execute the following command:

```
$ alias df="df -h"   # Creating alias
$ df
```

The output obtained is as follows:

```
Filesystem      Size  Used Avail Use% Mounted on
devtmpfs        3.8G     0  3.8G   0% /dev
tmpfs           3.8G  328K  3.8G   1% /dev/shm
tmpfs           3.8G  1.2M  3.8G   1% /run
tmpfs           3.8G     0  3.8G   0% /sys/fs/cgroup
/dev/sda1        38G   14G   23G  38% /
tmpfs           3.8G  292K  3.8G   1% /tmp
/dev/dm-0       197G   85G  103G  46% /home
tmpfs           767M     0  767M   0% /run/user/990
tmpfs           767M   36K  767M   1% /run/user/1000
```

We see that after creating alias of df -h to df, a default disk space is printed in a human-readable format.

Another useful example can be aliasing the rm command to rm -i. Using rm with the -i option asks the user for a confirmation before deleting them:

```
#!/bin/bash
# Filename: alias.sh
# Description: Creating alias of rm -i

touch /tmp/file.txt
rm /tmp/file.txt        # File gets deleted silently
touch /tmp/file.txt     # Creating again a file
alias rm="rm -i" # Creating alias of rm -i
rm /tmp/file.txt
```

The output after executing the preceding script is as follows:

```
rm: remove regular empty file '/tmp/file.txt'? Y
```

We can see that after alias creation, rm asks for a confirmation before deleting the /tmp/file.txt file.

Listing all aliases

To see the aliases that are already set for the current shell, use an alias without any argument or with the -p option:

```
$ alias
alias df='df -h'
alias egrep='egrep --color=auto'
alias fgrep='fgrep --color=auto'
alias grep='grep --color=auto'
alias l.='ls -d .* --color=auto'
alias ll='ls -l --color=auto'
alias ls='ls --color=auto'
alias vi='vim'
```

We can see that the df alias that we created still exists, along with the already other existing aliases.

Removing an alias

To remove an already existing alias, we can use the unalias shell builtin command:

```
$ unalias df  # Deletes df alias
$ alias -p  # Printing existing aliases
alias egrep='egrep --color=auto'
alias fgrep='fgrep --color=auto'
alias grep='grep --color=auto'
alias l.='ls -d .* --color=auto'
alias ll='ls -l --color=auto'
alias ls='ls --color=auto'
alias vi='vim'
```

We see that the df alias has been removed. To remove all aliases, use unalias with the a option:

```
$ unalias -a  # Delets all aliases for current shell
$ alias -p
```

We can see that all aliases have now been deleted.

pushd and popd

Both pushd and popd are shell builtin commands. The pushd command is used to save the current directory into a stack and move to a new directory. Furthermore, popd can be used to return back to the previous directory that is on top of the stack.

It is very useful when we have to switch between two directories frequently.

The syntax of using pushd is as follows:

```
pushd [directory]
```

If no directory is specified, pushd changes the directory to whatever is on the top of the stack.

The syntax of using popd is as follows:

```
popd
```

Using the popd switch, we can go back to the previous directory that is on top of the stack and pop that directory from stack.

The following example counts the number of files or directories in a specified directory until one level:

```
#!/bin/bash
# Filename: pushd_popd.sh
# Description: Count number of files and directories

echo "Enter a directory path"
read path

if [ -d $path ]
then
    pushd $path > /dev/null
    echo "File count in $path directory = 'ls | wc -l'"
    for f in 'ls'
    do
        if [ -d $f ]
        then
            pushd $f > /dev/null
            echo "File count in sub-directory $f = 'ls | wc -l'"
```

```
            popd > /dev/null
        fi
    done
    popd > /dev/null
else
    echo "$path is not a directory"
fi
```

The output after running the preceding script is as follows:

```
Enter a directory path
/usr/local
File count in /usr/local directory = 10
File count in sub-directory bin = 0
File count in sub-directory etc = 0
File count in sub-directory games = 0
File count in sub-directory include = 0
File count in sub-directory lib = 0
File count in sub-directory lib64 = 0
File count in sub-directory libexec = 0
File count in sub-directory sbin = 0
File count in sub-directory share = 3
File count in sub-directory src = 0
```

Summary

After reading this chapter, you should now be confident enough to write an effective shell script by using conditional statements, loops, and so on. Now, you can also write a modular and reusable code using the function in shell. Having the knowledge of exit code will help in knowing whether the command was executed successfully or not. You should also know a few more useful shell builtins such as alias, pushd, and popd.

In the next chapter, we will learn more about modularizing our script by knowing how to write a reusable shell script itself, which can be used in shell scripts. We will also see how we can debug our shell scripts to fix problems.

4
Modularizing and Debugging

In the real world, when you write code, you either maintain it forever or someone takes ownership of it later and makes changes into it. It is very important that you write a good quality shell script so that it's easier to maintain it further. It is also important that the shell script is bug-free in order to get the work done as expected. Scripts running on production systems are very critical because any error or wrong behavior of the script may cause minor or major damage. To solve such critical issues, it is important to get it fixed as soon as possible.

In this chapter, we will see how we can write modular and reusable code so that maintaining and updating our shell script application can be done quickly and without any hassle. We will also see how easily and quickly bugs in shell scripts can be solved using different debugging techniques. We will see how we can provide our users different choices for different tasks by providing support for command line options in a script. The knowledge of how to provide command line completion in a script will even increase the ease of using the script.

This chapter will cover the following topics in detail:

- Modularizing your scripts
- Passing command line parameters to script
- Debugging your scripts
- Command completion

Modularizing your scripts

While writing a shell script, there is one stage when we feel that a shell script file has become too big to read and manage. To avoid such a scenario in our shell script, it is very important to keep the script modular.

In order to keep the script modular and maintainable, you can do the following:

- Create functions instead of writing the same code again and again
- Write a common set of functions and variables in a separate script and then source to use it

We have already seen how to define and use a function in *Chapter 3*, *Effective Script Writing*. Here, we will see how to divide a bigger script into smaller shell script modules and then use them by sourcing. In other words, we can say creating libraries in bash.

Source to a script file

Source is a shell built in command that reads and executes a script file in the current shell environment. If a script calls a source on another script file, all functions and variables available in that file will be loaded for use in calling script.

Syntax

The syntax of using the source is as follows:

```
source <script filename> [arguments]
```

OR:

```
. <script filename> [arguments]
```

The script filename can be with or without a path name. If the absolute or relative path is provided, it will look only into that path. Otherwise, a filename will be searched in the directories specified in the PATH variable.

The arguments are treated as positional parameters to the script filename.

The exit status of the source command will be the exit code of the last command executed in the script filename. If the script filename doesn't exist or there is no permission, then the exit status will be 1.

Creating a shell script library

A library provides a collection of features that can be reused by another application without rewriting from scratch. We can create a library in shell by putting our functions and variables to be reused in a shell script file.

The following `shell_library.sh` script is an example of a shell library:

```
#!/bin/bash
# Filename: shell_library.sh
# Description: Demonstrating creation of library in shell

# Declare global variables
declare is_regular_file
declare is_directory_file

# Function to check file type
function file_type()
{
  is_regular_file=0
  is_directory_file=0
  if [ -f $1 ]
  then
    is_regular_file=1
  elif [ -d $1 ]
  then
    is_directory_file=1
  fi
}

# Printing regular file detail
function print_file_details()
{
    echo "Filename - $1"
    echo "Line count - `cat $1 | wc -l`"
    echo "Size - `du -h $1 | cut -f1`"
    echo "Owner - `ls -l $1 | tr -s ' '|cut -d ' ' -f3`"
    echo "Last modified date - `ls -l $1 | tr -s ' '|cut -d ' ' -f6,7`"
}

# Printing directory details
function print_directory_details()
{
```

```
    echo "Directory Name - $1"
    echo "File Count in directory - `ls $1|wc -l`"
    echo "Owner - `ls -ld $1 | tr -s ' '|cut -d ' ' -f3`"
    echo "Last modified date - `ls -ld $1 | tr -s ' '
-f6,7`"
}
```

The preceding `shell_library.sh` shell script contains the `is_regular_file` and `is_directory_file` global variables that can be used to know whether a given file is a regular file or directory after invoking the `file_type()` function. Furthermore, depending upon the type of the file, useful detailed information can be printed.

Loading a shell script library

Creating shell libraries are of no use unless it is used in another shell script.
We can either use a shell script library directly in shell or within another script file.
To load a shell script library, we will use the source command or. (period character) followed by shell script library.

Calling a shell library in bash

To use the `shell_library.sh` script file in shell, we can do the following:

$ source shell_library.sh

OR:

$. shell_library.sh

Calling any of them will make functions and variables available for use in the current shell:

```
$ file_type /usr/bin
$ echo $is_directory_file
1
$ echo $is_regular_file
0
$ if [ $is_directory_file -eq 1 ]; then print_directory_details /usr/
bin; fi
Directory Name - /usr/bin
File Count in directory - 2336
Owner - root
Last modified date - Jul 12
```

When the `file_type /usr/bin` command is executed, the `file_type()` function with the `/usr/bin` parameter will be called. As a result, the global variable `is_directory_file` or `is_regular_file` will get set to 1 (true), depending upon the type of the `/usr/bin` path. Using the shell `if` condition, we test whether the `is_directory_file` variable is set to 1 or not. If set to 1, then call the `print_directory_details()` function with `/usr/bin` as a parameter to print its details.

Calling shell library in another shell script

The following example explains the usage of the shell library in a shell script file:

```
#!/bin/bash
# Filename: shell_library_usage.sh
# Description: Demonstrating shell library usage in shell script

# Print details of all files/directories in a directory
echo "Enter path of directory"
read dir

# Loading shell_library.sh module
. $PWD/shell_library.sh

# Check if entered pathname is a directory
# If directory, then print files/directories details inside it
file_type $dir
if [ $is_directory_file -eq 1 ]
then
    pushd $dir > /dev/null       # Save current directory and cd to
$dir
    for file in `ls`
    do
      file_type $file
      if [ $is_directory_file -eq 1 ]
      then
        print_directory_details $file
        echo
      elif [ $is_regular_file -eq 1 ]
      then
        print_file_details $file
        echo
      fi
    done
fi
```

The output after running the `shell_library_usage.sh` script is as follows:

```
$ sh  shell_library_usage.sh  # Few outputs from /usr directory
Enter path of directory
/usr
Directory Name - bin
File Count in directory - 2336
Owner - root
Last modified date - Jul 12

Directory Name - games
File Count in directory - 0
Owner - root
Last modified date - Aug 16

Directory Name - include
File Count in directory - 172
Owner - root
Last modified date - Jul 12

Directory Name - lib
File Count in directory - 603
Owner - root
Last modified date - Jul 12

Directory Name - lib64
File Count in directory - 3380
Owner - root
Last modified date - Jul 12

Directory Name - libexec
File Count in directory - 170
Owner - root
Last modified date - Jul 7
```

To load a shell script library, use `source` or `.` followed by `script_filename`.

Both source and `.` (period character) execute a script in the current shell. `./script` is not the same as `. script` because `./script` executes the script in a subshell, while `. script` executes in a shell from where it was invoked.

Passing command line parameters to script

So far, we have seen the usage of the commands such as grep, head, ls, cat, and many more. These commands also support passing arguments to a command via a command line. Some of command line arguments are input files, output files, and options. Arguments are provided as per output needs. For example, ls -l filename is executed to get a long listing output, while ls -R filename is used to display recursively the contents of a directory.

Shell script also supports providing command line arguments that we can process further by a shell script.

The command line arguments can be given as follows:

`<script_file> arg1 arg2 arg3 … argN`

Here, script_file is a shell script file to be executed, and arg1, arg2, arg3, argN, and so on, are command line parameters.

Reading arguments in scripts

Command line arguments are passed to a shell script as positional parameters. So, arg1 will be accessed in a script as $1, arg2 as $2, and so on.

The following shell demonstrates the usage of the command line arguments:

```
#!/bin/bash
# Filename: command_line_arg.sh
# Description: Accessing command line parameters in shell script

# Printing first, second and third command line parameters"
echo "First command line parameter = $1"
echo "Second command line parameter = $2"
echo "Third command line parameter = $3"
```

The following output is obtained after running the command_line_arg.sh script with arguments:

```
$  sh command_line_arg.sh Linux Shell Scripting
First command line parameter = Linux
Second command line parameter = Shell
Third command line parameter = Scripting
```

The following table shows special variables that are useful to get more information about command line parameters:

Special variables	Description
$#	Number of the command line arguments
$*	Complete set of command line arguments in a single string—that is, '$1 $2 ... $n'
$@	Complete set of command line arguments, but each argument is enclosed in separate quotes—that is, '$1' '$2' ... '$n'
$0	Name of the shell script itself
$1, $1, ... $N	Refers to argument1, argument2, ..., argumentN, respectively

Using $# in a script to check the number of command line arguments will be very helpful to process arguments further.

The following is another shell script example that takes command line arguments:

```
#!/bin/bash
# Filename: command_line_arg2.sh
# Description: Creating directories in /tmp

# Check if at least 1 argument is passed in command line
if [ $# -lt 1 ]
then
   echo "Specify minimum one argument to create directory"
   exit 1
else
   pushd /tmp > /dev/null
   echo "Directory to be created are: $@"
   mkdir $@       # Accessing all command line arguments
fi
```

The following output is obtained after executing the command_line_arg2.sh script:

```
$ sh command_line_arg2.sh a b
Directory to be created are: a b
$ sh command_line_arg2.sh
Specify minimum one argument to create directory
```

Shifting command line arguments

To shift command line arguments towards the left, the `shift` built in can be used. The syntax is as follows:

```
shift N
```

Here, `N` is the number of arguments by which it can shift to the left.

For example, suppose the current command line arguments are arg1, arg2, arg3, arg4 and arg5. They can be accessed in a shell script as $1, $2, $3, $4, and $5, respectively; the $# value is 5. When we call `shift 3`, arguments get shifted by 3. Now, $1 contains arg4 and $2 contains arg5. Also, the $# value is now 2.

The following shell script demonstrates the usage of `shift`:

```
#!/bin/bash
# Filename: shift_argument.sh
# Description: Usage of shift shell builtin

echo "Length of command line arguments = $#"
echo "Arguments are:"
echo "\$1 = $1, \$2 = $2, \$3 = $3, \$4 = $4, \$5 = $5, \$6 = $6"
echo "Shifting arguments by 3"
shift 3
echo "Length of command line arguments after 3 shift = $#"
echo "Arguments after 3 shifts are"
echo "\$1 = $1, \$2 = $2, \$3 = $3, \$4 = $4, \$5 = $5, \$6 = $6"
```

The following output is obtained after running the `shift_argument.sh` script with the arguments a b c d e f:

```
$ sh shift_argument.sh a b c d e f
Length of command line arguments = 6
Arguments are:
$1 = a, $2 = b, $3 = c, $4 = d, $5 = e, $6 = f
Shifting arguments by 3
Length of command line arguments after 3 shift = 3
Arguments after 3 shifts are
$1 = d, $2 = e, $3 = f, $4 = , $5 = , $6 =
```

Processing command line options in a script

Providing command line options make shell scripts more interactive. From the command line arguments, we can also parse options for further processing by a shell script.

The following shell script shows the command line usage with options:

```
#!/bin/bash
# Filename: myprint.sh
# Description: Showing how to create command line options in shell
script

function display_help()
{
  echo "Usage: myprint [OPTIONS] [arg ...]"
  echo "--help  Display help"
  echo "--version     Display version of script"
  echo  "--print      Print arguments"
}

function display_version()
{
  echo "Version of shell script application is 0.1"
}

function myprint()
{
  echo "Arguments are: $*"
}

# Parsing command line arguments

if [ "$1" != "" ]
then
    case $1 in
        --help )
            display_help
            exit 1
            ;;
        --version )
            display_version
            exit 1
            ;;
```

```
        --print )
            shift
            myprint $@
            exit 1
            ;;
    *)
    display_help
    exit 1
    esac
fi
```

The following output is obtained after executing the `myprint.sh` script:

```
$ sh myprint.sh --help
Usage: myprint [OPTIONS] [arg ...]
--help      Display help
--version      Display version of script
--print        Print arguments
$ sh myprint.sh --version
Version of shell script application is 0.1
$ sh myprint.sh --print Linux Shell Scripting
Arguments are: Linux Shell Scripting
```

Debugging your scripts

We write different shell scripts to perform different tasks. Have you ever encountered any errors while executing a shell script? The answer would be mostly yes! This is to be expected as it is practically impossible to always write perfect shell scripts, without errors or bugs.

For example, the following shell script is a buggy script while execution:

```
#!/bin/bash
# Filename: buggy_script.sh
# Description: Demonstrating a buggy script

a=12 b=8
if [ a -gt $b ]
then
  echo "a is greater than b"
else
  echo "b is greater than a"
fi
```

The following output is obtained after executing `buggy_script.sh`:

```
$ sh buggy_script.sh
buggy_script.sh: line 6: [: a: integer expression expected
b is greater than a
```

From the output, we see that the error `[: a: integer expression expected` occurred at line 6. It's not always possible to know the reason of the error by just looking into an error message, especially when seeing an error for the first time. Also, looking manually into the code and rectifying an error is difficult when dealing with a lengthy shell script.

To overcome all kinds of troubles while resolving an error or bug in a shell script, it's preferred to debug code. Debugging ways to debug a shell script are as follows:

- Using `echo` in an expected buggy area of a script to print the contents of the variables or commands to be executed
- Debugging an entire script using -x while running a script
- Debugging a section of a script using set builtin command with the -x and +x options inside the script

Debugging using echo

The `echo` command is very useful as it prints whatever arguments are provided to it. When we encounter an error while executing a script, we know the line number with an error message. In such a case, we can use `echo` to print what is going to be executed before the actual execution.

In our previous example, `buggy_script.sh`, we got an error at line 6 — that is `if [ a -gt $b ]` — while execution. We can use the `echo` statement to print what is actually going to be executed at line 6. The following shell script adds `echo` in line 6, to see what will be executed finally at line 6:

```
#!/bin/bash
# Filename: debugging_using_echo.sh
# Description: Debugging using echo

a=12 b=8
echo "if [ a -gt $b ]"
exit
if [ a -gt $b ]
then
```

```
   echo "a is greater than b"
else
   echo "b is greater than a"
fi
```

We will now execute the `debugging_using_echo.sh` script as follows:

$ sh debugging_using_echo.sh

if [a -gt 8]

We can see that the character a is getting compared with 8, while we were expecting the value of the variable a. This means that, by mistake, we forgot to use $ with a to extract the value of the variable a.

Debugging an entire script using -x

Using echo to debug is easy if the script is small, or if we know where exactly the problem is. Another disadvantage of using echo is that every time we make changes, we will have to open a shell script and modify the echo command accordingly. After debugging, we will have to remember to delete the extra echo lines added for the purposes of debugging.

To overcome these problems, bash provides the -x option that can be used while executing a shell script. Running a script with the -x option runs a script in the debug mode. This prints all the commands that are going to be executed along with the output of the script.

Consider the following shell script as an example:

```
#!/bin/bash
# Filename : debug_entire_script.sh
# Description: Debugging entire shell script using -x

# Creating diretcories in /tmp
dir1=/tmp/$1
dir2=/tmp/$2
mkdir $dir1 $dir2
ls -ld $dir1
ls -ld $dir2
rmdir $dir1
rmdir $dir2
```

Now, we will run the preceding script as follows:

```
$ sh debug_entire_script.sh pkg1
mkdir: cannot create directory '/tmp/': File exists
drwxrwxr-x. 2 skumari skumari 40 Jul 14 01:47 /tmp/pkg1
drwxrwxrwt. 23 root root 640 Jul 14 01:47 /tmp/
rmdir: failed to remove '/tmp/': Permission denied
```

It gives an error that the /tmp/ directory already exists. By looking into the error, we can't say why it is trying to create the /tmp directory. To trace the entire code, we can run the debug_entire_script.sh script with the -x option:

```
$ sh -x debug_entire_script.sh pkg1
+ dir1=/tmp/pkg1
+ dir2=/tmp/
+ mkdir /tmp/pkg1 /tmp/
mkdir: cannot create directory '/tmp/': File exists
+ ls -ld /tmp/pkg1
drwxrwxr-x. 2 skumari skumari 40 Jul 14 01:47 /tmp/pkg1
+ ls -ld /tmp/
drwxrwxrwt. 23 root root 640 Jul 14 01:47 /tmp/
+ rmdir /tmp/pkg1
+ rmdir /tmp/
rmdir: failed to remove '/tmp/': Permission denied
```

We can see that dir2 is /tmp/. This means that no input is given to create the second directory.

Using the -v option along with -x makes debugging even more verbose because -v displays input lines as it is:

```
$ sh -xv debug_entire_script.sh pkg1
#!/bin/bash
# Filename : debug_entire_script.sh
# Description: Debugging entire shell script using -x

# Creating diretcories in /tmp
dir1=/tmp/$1
+ dir1=/tmp/pkg1
dir2=/tmp/$2
```

```
+ dir2=/tmp/
mkdir $dir1 $dir2
+ mkdir /tmp/pkg1 /tmp/
mkdir: cannot create directory '/tmp/': File exists
ls -ld $dir1
+ ls -ld /tmp/pkg1
drwxrwxr-x. 2 skumari skumari 40 Jul 14 01:47 /tmp/pkg1
ls -ld $dir2
+ ls -ld /tmp/
drwxrwxrwt. 23 root root 640 Jul 14 01:47 /tmp/
rmdir $dir1
+ rmdir /tmp/pkg1
rmdir $dir2
+ rmdir /tmp/
rmdir: failed to remove '/tmp/': Permission denied
```

With verbose output, it is quite clear that the dir1 and dir2 variables are expecting a command line argument. So, two arguments must be provided from a command line:

```
$ sh debug_entire_script.sh pkg1 pkg2
drwxrwxr-x. 2 skumari skumari 40 Jul 14 01:50 /tmp/pkg1
drwxrwxr-x. 2 skumari skumari 40 Jul 14 01:50 /tmp/pkg2
```

Now, the script works without any errors.

 Instead of passing the -xv options to bash from a command line, we can add it in the shebang line in the script file—that is, #!/bin/bash -xv.

Debugging sections of a script using the set options

To debug a shell script, it's not necessary to debug the entire script all the time. Sometimes, debugging a partial script is more useful and time-saving. We can achieve partial debugging in a shell script using the set builtin command:

```
set -x   (Start debugging from here)
set +x   (End debugging here)
```

We can use set +x and set -x inside a shell script at multiple places depending upon the need. When a script is executed, commands in between them are printed along with the output.

Consider the following shell script as an example:

```
#!/bin/bash
# Filename: eval.sh
# Description: Evaluating arithmetic expression

a=23
b=6
expr $a + $b
expr $a - $b
expr $a * $b
```

Executing this script gives the following output:

```
$ sh eval.sh
29
17
expr: syntax error
```

We get the syntax error with an expression that is most likely the third expression — that is, expr $a * $b.

To debug, we will use set -x before and set +x after expr $a * $b.

Another script partial_debugging.sh with partial debugging is as follows:

```
#!/bin/bash
# Filename: partial_debugging.sh
# Description: Debugging part of script of eval.sh

a=23
b=6
expr $a + $b

expr $a - $b

set -x
expr $a * $b
set +x
```

The following output is obtained after executing the `partial_debugging.sh` script:

```
$  sh partial_debugging.sh
29
17
+ expr 23 eval.sh partial_debugging.sh 6
expr: syntax error
+ set +x
```

From the preceding output, we can see that `expr $a * $b` is executed as `expr 23 eval.sh partial_debugging.sh 6`. This means, instead of doing multiplication, bash is expanding the behavior of `*` as anything available in the current directory. So, we need to escape the behavior of the character `*` from getting expanded—that is, `expr $a \* $b`.

The following script `eval_modified.sh` is a modified form of the `eval.sh` script:

```
#!/bin/bash
# Filename: eval_modified.sh
# Description: Evaluating arithmetic expression

a=23
b=6
expr $a + $b
expr $a - $b
expr $a \* $b
```

Now, the output of running `eval_modified.sh` will be as follows:

```
$  sh eval_modified.sh
29
17
138
```

The script runs perfectly now without any errors.

Other than what we have learned in debugging, you can also use the `bashdb` debugger for even better debugging of the shell script. The source code and documentation for `bashdb` can be found at `http://bashdb.sourceforge.net/`.

Command completion

While working on a command line, everyone has to do a common task such as typing, which includes commands, its options, input/output file path, and other arguments. Sometimes, we write a wrong command name because of a spelling error in the command name. Also, typing a long file path will be very difficult to remember. For example, if we want to look recursively into the contents of a directory present at the path `/dir1/dir2/dir3/dir4/dir5/dir6`, we will have to run the following command:

```
$ ls -R /dir1/dir2/dir3/dir4/dir5/dir6
```

We can see that the path of this directory is very long and there is a high chance of making an error while typing the full path. Due to these issues, working on a command line will take a longer time than expected.

To solve all these problems, shell supports a very nice feature called command completion. Along with the other shell, bash also has a very good support of command completion.

Most of the Linux distributions, for example, Fedora, Ubuntu, Debian, and CentOS have a pre-installed bash completion for core commands. If not available, it can be downloaded using the corresponding distribution package manager with the package name `bash-completion`.

Command completion in shell allows you to autocomplete the rest of the characters of the partially typed command, suggesting possible options associated with the given command. It also suggests and autocompletes the partially typed file path.

To enable autocompletion feature in bash, the *Tab* key is used. While typing a command, a single TAB autocompletes the command if the single command matches, and double [TAB] lists all the possible commands starting with a partially typed command.

For example:

```
$ gr[TAB]       # Nothing happens
$ gre[TAB]       # Autocompletes to grep
$ grep[TAB][TAB]  # Lists commands installed in system and starts with
grep
grep           grep-changelog  grepdiff
```

Now, suppose we want to see the contents of the `/usr/share/man/` directory, we will have to type `ls /usr/share/man/`. Using bash completion, type the following command:

```
$ ls /u[TAB]/sh[TAB]/man
```

Bash completion will auto-complete the missing partial path and the command will become:

```
$ ls /usr/share/man
```

Managing bash completion with complete

The `complete` is a shell builtin that can be used to see the available bash completion specification for the available commands in a system. It is also used to modify, delete, and create bash completion.

Viewing the existing bash completion

To know the existing bash completion, use the `complete` command with or without the `-p` option:

```
$ complete -p
```

The following are some of the outputs of the preceding command:

```
complete cat   # No completion output
complete -F _longopt grep  # Completion as files from current directory
complete -d pushd  # Completion as directories from current directory
complete -c which  # Completion as list of all available commands
```

To see bash completion on these commands, type the following command:

This lists all files/directories, including hidden files/directories:

```
$ grep [TAB][TAB]
```

This lists all files/directories, including hidden files/directories:

```
$ cat [TAB][TAB]
```

This tries to list all the available commands in a system. Pressing *y* will display commands and *n* will display nothing.

```
$ complete -c which [TAB][TAB]
    Display all 3205 possibilities? (y or n)
```

Modifying default bash completion behavior

We can also modify the existing bash completion behavior of a given command using the complete shell builtin command.

The following command is used to change the behavior of the `which` command to not display any options:

```
$ complete which
$ which [TAB][TAB]  # No auto completion option will be shown
```

The following command is used to change the `ls` command tab behavior to show only the directories list as bash completion:

```
$ ls ~/[TAB][TAB]    # Displays directories and file as  auto-completion
file1.sh file2.txt dir1/ dir2/ dir3/
$ complete -d ls
$ ls ~/[TAB][TAB]    # Displays only directory name as  auto-completion
dir1/ dir2/ dir3/
```

Removing bash completion specification

We can remove bash completion specification for a command using the shell builtin `complete` with the `-r` option.

The syntax is as follows:

```
complete -r command_name
```

Consider the following as an example:

```
$ complete | grep which  # Viewing bash completion specification for
which
complete -c which
$ complete -r which    # Removed bash completion specification for which
$ complete | grep which  # No output
```

If no `command_name` is given as an argument to complete -r, all the completion specifications are removed:

```
$ complete -r
$ complete
```

Writing bash completion for your own application

The bash-completion package doesn't provide autocompletion feature for any external tools. Suppose that we want to create a tool that has multiple options and arguments. To add a bash-completion feature to its options, we will have to create our own bash completion file and source into it.

For example, package managers such as `dnf` and `apt-get` have its own bash completion file to support autocompletion for its options:

```
$ dnf up[TAB] [TAB]
update        updateinfo   update-to   upgrade      upgrade-to
$ apt-get up[TAB] [TAB]
update upgrade
```

Consider the following shell script as an example:

```bash
#!/bin/bash
# Filename: bash_completion_example.sh
# Description: Example demonstrating bash completion feature for
command options

function help()
{
  echo "Usage: print [OPTIONS] [arg ...]"
  echo "-h|--help    Display help"
  echo "-v|--version Display version of script"
  echo "-p|--print    Print arguments"
}

function version()
{
  echo "Version of shell script application is 0.1"
}
```

```
function print()
{
  echo "Arguments are: $*"
}

# Parsing command line arguments

while [ "$1" != "" ]
do
    case $1 in
         -h | --help )
             help
             exit 1
             ;;
         -v | --version )
             version
             exit 1
             ;;
         -p | --print )
             shift
             print $@
             exit 1
             ;;
     *)
     help
      exit 1
    esac
  done
```

To know about the supported options in bash_completion_example.sh, we will run the --help option:

```
$ chmod +x bash_completion_example.sh    # Adding execute permission to
script
$ ./bash_completion_example.sh --help
Usage: print [OPTIONS] [arg ...]
-h|--help    Display help
-v|--version Display version of script
-p|--print    Print arguments
```

So, the supported options are -h, --help, -v, --version, -p, and --print.

To write bash completion, information of the following bash internal variables are required:

Bash variables	Description
COMP_WORDS	An array of words that is typed on the command line
COMP_CWORD	An index of the word containing the current cursor position.
COMPREPLY	An array that holds the completion results that get displayed after pressing [TAB][TAB]

The compgen is a shell builtin command that displays the possible completions depending on the options. It is used in shell functions to generate possible completions.

An example of bash completion

A bash-completion file for our shell script bash_completion_example will be as follows:

```
# Filename: bash_completion_example
# Description: Bash completion for bash_completion_example.sh

_bash_completion_example()
{
    # Declaring local variables
    local cur prev opts
    # An array variable storing the possible completions
    COMPREPLY=()
    # Save current word typed on command line in  cur variable
    cur="${COMP_WORDS[COMP_CWORD]}"
    # Saving previous word typed on command line in prev variable
    prev="${COMP_WORDS[COMP_CWORD-1]}"
    # Save all options provided by application in variable opts
    opts="-h -v -p --help --verbose --print"

    # Checking "${cur} == -*" means that perform completion only if
current
    # word starts with a dash (-), which suggest that user is trying
to complete an option.
    # Variable COMPREPLY contains the match of the current word
"${cur}" against the list
```

```
    if [[ ${cur} == -* ]] ; then
        COMPREPLY=( $(compgen -W "${opts}" -- ${cur}) )
        return 0
    fi
}


# Register _bash_completion_example to provide completion
# on running script bash_completion_example.sh
complete -F _bash_completion_example ./bash_completion_example.sh
```

As per convention, a bash-completion function name should start with an underscore (_) followed by the name of the application—that is, _bash_completion_example. Furthermore, we reset the bash variable COMPREPLY to clean up any previous left out data. Then, we declare and set the cur variable to the current word of the command line and the prev variable to the previous word in the command line. Another variable opts is declared and initialized with all the options that are recognized by an application; in our case, they are -h -v -p --help --verbose -print. The condition if [[${cur} == -*]] checks whether the current word is equal to -* because our option starts with - followed by any other character. If true, then display all the matching options using the compgen shell builtin with the -W option.

Running the created bash completion

In order to run the created bash completion, the easiest way is to source into source bash_completion_example shell script and then run the script or command:

```
$ source ./bash_completion_example
Now,  execute shell script:
$ ./bash_completion_example.sh - [TAB] [TAB]
-h          --help      -p          --print     -v          --verbose
$ ./bash_completion_example.sh -- [TAB] [TAB]
--help      --print     --verbose
$  ./bash_completion_example.sh --p [TAB]
```

Here, --p [TAB] gets auto-completed to --print.

Summary

After reading this chapter, you should now able to write a shell script that can be easy to maintain and modify by others. Now, you know how to use an existing shell script library in your own script by using the `source` command. You also got familiarity with fixing errors and bugs in a shell script by making use of the different debugging techniques. You should also know how to write a script by taking command line arguments and providing bash completion features for it.

In the next chapter, we will see how to view, change, create, and delete environment variables in order to meet the requirement of running our applications.

Customizing the Environment

In a default system, we get certain settings that are preconfigured. As time progresses, we often feel the need to modify some of the default settings provided. Similar needs arise when we are working in a shell to get things done, for example, modifying the environment according to the needs of the application. Some of the features are so irresistible that we may need them every time, for example, the editor of our choice used by an application. While working on an important task, it may happen that we forget a command that we used a few days ago. In such cases, we try to recall that command as soon as possible to get work done. If we can't remember, we consume time and effort searching on the Internet or in text books for the exact command and syntax.

In this chapter, we will see how, by adding or changing the existing environment variables, we can modify the environment as per our application needs. We will also see how a user can modify the `.bashrc`, `.bash_profile`, and `.bash_logout` files to make the setting changes available permanently. We will see how we can search and modify the history of previously executed commands. We will also see how to run multiple tasks from a single shell and manage them together.

This chapter will cover the following topics in detail:

- Knowing the default environment
- Modifying the shell environment
- Using bash startup files
- Knowing your history
- Managing tasks

Knowing the default environment

Setting up a proper environment is very important for running a process. An environment consists of environment variables that may or may not have a default value set. The required environment is set by modifying the existing environment variables or creating new environment variables. Environment variables are exported variables that are available to the current process and also its child processes. In *Chapter 1, The Beginning of the Scripting Journey*, we learned about some of the builtin shell variables that can be used in our application as environment variables to set the environment.

Viewing a shell environment

To view the current environment in the shell, we can use the printenv or env commands. Environment variables may have no value, a single value, or a multiple value set. If multiple values exist, each value is separated by a colon (:).

printenv

We can use printenv to print the value associated with a given environment variable. The syntax is as follows:

```
$ printenv [VARIABLE]
```

Consider the following as examples:

```
$ printenv SHELL     # Prints which shell is being used
/bin/bash
$ printenv PWD     # Present working directory
/home/foo/Documents
$ printenv HOME     # Prints user's home directory
/home/foo
$ printenv PATH     # Path where command to be executed is searched
/usr/lib64/qt-3.3/bin:/usr/lib64/ccache:/bin:/usr/bin:/usr/local/bin:/
usr/local/sbin:/usr/sbin:/home/foo
$ printenv USER HOSTNAME   # Prints value of both environment variables
foo
localhost
```

If no VARIABLE is specified, printenv prints all environment variables as follows:

```
$ printenv  # Prints all environment variables available to current shell
```

env

We can also use the env command to view environment variables as follows:

```
$ env
```

This displays all environment variables defined for a given shell.

 To view value(s) of a specific environment variable, the echo command can also be used followed by an environment variable name prefixed with a dollar symbol ($). For example, echo $SHELL.

Differences between shell and environment variables

Both shell and environment variables are variables that are accessible and set for a given shell that may be used by an application or a command running in that shell. However, there are a few differences between them, which are set out in the following table:

Shell variables	Environment variables
Both local and exported variables are shell variables	Exported shell variables are environment variables
The set builtin command is used to see the name and corresponding value of a shell variable	The env or printenv command is used to see the name and corresponding value of an environment variable
Local shell variables are not available for use by their child shells	Child shells inherit all environment variables present in the parent shell
A shell variable is created by specifying a variable name on the left and value(s) separated by a colon (:) on the right-hand side of an equal operator (=)	An environment variable can be created by prefixing an export shell built - in command to the existing shell variable, or while creating a new shell variable

Modifying a shell environment

When a new shell is launched, it has the initial environment set that will be used by any application or command that gets executed in a given shell. We now know that the env or setenv shell builtin command can be used to view which environment variables are set for this shell. The shell also provides the capability to modify the current environment. We can also modify the current bash environment by creating, modifying, or deleting environment variables.

Creating environment variables

To create a new environment variable in a shell, the export shell builtin command is used.

For example, we will create a new environment variable ENV_VAR1:

```
$ env | grep ENV_VAR1  # Verifying that ENV_VAR1 doesn't exist
$ export ENV_VAR1='New environment variable'
```

A new environment variable with the name ENV_VAR1 is created. To view a new environment variable, we can call the printenv or env command:

```
$ env | grep ENV_VAR1
ENV_VAR1=New environment variable
$ printenv ENV_VAR1     # Viewing value of ENV_VAR1 environment variable
New environment variable
```

We can also use the echo command to print the value of an environment variable:

```
$ echo $ENV_VAR1  # Printing value of ENV_VAR1 environment variable
New environment variable
```

A local shell variable can also be exported further as an environment variable. As an example, we will create the ENV_VAR2 and LOCAL_VAR1 variables:

```
$ ENV_VAR2='Another environment variable'
$ LOCAL_VAR1='Local variable'
$ env | grep ENV_VAR2 # Verifying if ENV_VAR2 is an environment variable
```

No environment variable is found with the name ENV_VAR2. This is because while creating ENV_VAR2, it wasn't exported. Therefore, it will be created as a local variable of a shell:

```
$ set | grep ENV_VAR2
ENV_VAR2='Another environment variable'
$ set | grep  LOCAL_VAR1
LOCAL_VAR1='Local variable'
```

Now, to make the ENV_VAR2 shell variable as an environment variable, we can use the export command:

```
$ export ENV_VAR2    # Becomes environment variable
$ printenv ENV_VAR2    # Checking of  ENV_VAR2 is an environment variable
Another environment variable
$ printenv LOCAL_VAR1
```

The variable LOCAL_VAR1 is not an environment variable.

One of the important features of environment variables is that it is available to all of its child shells. We can see this in the following example:

```
$ bash  # creating a new bash shell
$ env | grep ENV_VAR2  # Checking if  ENV_VAR2 is available in child shell
ENV_VAR2=Another environment variable
$ env | grep ENV_VAR1
ENV_VAR1=New environment variable
$ env | grep LOCAL_VAR1
```

We can see that the environment variables from a parent shell got inherited by a child shell—for example, ENV_VAR1, ENV_VAR2—while the local variable, such as LOCAL_VAR1, remains available only to a shell in which the variable was created.

Modifying environment variables

Shell provides flexibility for modifying any existing environment variable. For example, consider the HOME environment variable. By default, the HOME environment variable contains the path of the current logged in user's home directory:

```
$ printenv HOME
/home/foo
$ pwd     # Checking current working directory
/tmp
$ cd $HOME     # Should change directory to /home/foo
$ pwd     # Check now current working directory
/home/foo
```

Now, we will modify the HOME environment variable value to /tmp:

```
$ HOME=/tmp     # Modifying HOME environment variable
$ printenv HOME     # Checking value of HOME environment variable
/tmp
$ cd $HOME     # Changing directory to what $HOME contains
$ pwd     # Checking current working directory
/tmp
```

We can also append a value to an environment variable. To do this, make sure the new value is separated with a colon (:). For example, consider the PATH environment variable:

```
$ printenv PATH
usr/lib64/ccache:/bin:/usr/bin:/usr/local/bin:/usr/local/sbin:/usr/sbin:/
home/foo/.local/bin:/home/foo/bin
```

Now, we want to add a new path to the PATH variable—for example, /home/foo/projects/bin—so that, while looking for a program or command, the shell can search the specified path too. To append a path to the PATH environment variable, use a colon (:) followed with a new path name:

```
$ PATH=$PATH:/home/foo/projects/bin   # Appends new path
$ printenv PATH
usr/lib64/ccache:/bin:/usr/bin:/usr/local/bin:/usr/local/sbin:/usr/sbin:/
home/foo/.local/bin:/home/foo/bin:/home/foo/projects/bin
```

We can see that the new path has been appended to the existing values of the PATH variable.

We can also append multiple values to an environment variable; for that, each value should be separated by a colon (:).

For example, we will add two more application paths to the PATH variable:

```
$ PATH=$PATH:/home/foo/project1/bin:PATH:/home/foo/project2/bin
$ printenv PATH
usr/lib64/ccache:/bin:/usr/bin:/usr/local/bin:/usr/local/sbin:/usr/sbin:/
home/foo/.local/bin:/home/foo/bin:/home/foo/projects/bin:/home/foo/
project1/bin:PATH:/home/foo/project2/bin
```

The two new paths, /home/foo/project1/bin and /home/foo/project2/bin, have been added to the PATH variable.

Deleting environment variables

We can delete or reset a value of an environment variable using the unset shell builtin command.

For example, we will create an environment variable called ENV1:

```
$ export ENV1='My environment variable'
$ env | grep ENV1  # Checking if ENV1 environment variable exist
ENV1=My environment variable
$ unset ENV1    # Deleting ENV1 environment variable
$ env | grep ENV1
```

The environment variable ENV1 gets deleted by the unset command. Now, to reset an environment variable, assign it a blank value:

```
$ export ENV2='Another environment variable'
$ env | grep ENV2
ENV2=Another environment variable
$ ENV2=''    # Reset ENV2 to blank
$ env | grep ENV2
ENV2=
```

Using bash startup files

Until now, to perform a task or set anything for a given shell, we had to execute the needed commands in a shell. One of the main limitations to this approach is that the same configuration won't be available in a new shell. In a lot of cases, a user may want that whenever he or she launches a new shell, whereas instead a new customized configuration on top of the default configuration is available for use. For customizing bash, three files are available in a user's home directory that get executed by default whenever a user launches a new bash. These files are bashrc, .bash_profile, and .bash_logout.

.bashrc

In a graphical system, mostly a non-login shell is used by a user. To run a non-login shell, we don't need the login credentials. Starting a shell in a graphical system provides a non-login shell. When a bash is invoked in non-login mode, the ~/.bashrc file is invoked and the configuration available in it is executed and applied in any bash shell being launched. Settings that are needed in both the login and non-login shell are kept in the ~/.bashrc file.

For example, on a Fedora 22 system default, the ~/.bashrc file looks as follows:

```
# .bashrc

# Source global definitions
if [ -f /etc/bashrc ]; then
        . /etc/bashrc
fi

# Uncomment the following line if you don't like systemctl's auto
paging feature:
# export SYSTEMD_PAGER=

# User specific aliases and functions
```

Any addition done in ~/.bashrc will be reflected only to the current user's bash shell. We can see that the .bashrc file also checks whether the etc/bashrc file is available. If available, that gets executed too. The /etc/bashrc file contains configuration applied to a bash shell for all users—that is, systemwide. Sysadmin can modify the /etc/bashrc file if any configuration needs to be applied to all users' bash shells.

The file /etc/bashrc also looks into the script files available in /etc/profile.d, which can be confirmed by the following code snippet taken from the /etc/bashrc file:

```
for i in /etc/profile.d/*.sh; do
      if [ -r "$i" ]; then
          if [ "$PS1" ]; then
               . "$i"
```

The following example shows a modified .bashrc file. Name this file custom_bashrc:

```
# custom_bashrc

# Source global definitions
if [ -f /etc/bashrc ]; then
      . /etc/bashrc
fi

# Uncomment the following line if you don't like systemctl's auto-
paging feature:
# export SYSTEMD_PAGER=

# User added settings
# Adding aliases
alias rm='rm -i'  # Prompt before every removal
alias cp='cp -i'  # Prompts before overwrite
alias df='df -h'  # Prints size in human readable format
alias ll='ls -l'  # Long listing of file

# Exporting environment variables
# Setting and exporting LD_LIBRARY_PATH variable
export LD_LIBRARY_PATH=$LD_LIBRARY_PATH:~/libs
# Setting number of commands saved in history file to 10000
export HISTFILESIZE=10000

# Defining functions
# Function to calculate size of current directory
function current_directory_size()
{
echo -n "Current directory is $PWD with total used space "
du -chs $PWD 2> /dev/null | grep total | cut -f1
}
```

The `LD_LIBRARY_PATH` environment variable is used to give the runtime shared library loader (`ld.so`) an extra set of directories to look for when searching for shared libraries. You can learn more about the shared library at `http://tldp.org/HOWTO/Program-Library-HOWTO/shared-libraries.html`.

Make a backup of your original `~/.bashrc` file before modifying it:

```
$ cp ~/.bashrc ~/.bashrc.bak
```

Now, copy the `custom_bashrc` file to `~/.bashrc`:

```
$ cp custom_bashrc ~/.bashrc
```

To apply modified settings, open a new bash shell. To apply a new `.bashrc` in the same bash shell, you can source into a new `~/.bashrc` file:

```
$ source ~/.bashrc
```

We can check whether the new settings are available or not:

```
$ ll /home  # Using alias ll which we created

    total 24
    drwx------.  2 root     root    16384 Jun 11 00:46 lost+found
    drwx--x---+ 41 foo  foo      4096  Aug  3 12:57 foo

$ alias  # To view aliases

    alias cp='cp -i'
    alias df='df -h'
    alias ll='ls -l'
    alias ls='ls --color=auto'
    alias rm='rm -i'
    alias vi='vim'
```

The `alias` command displays aliases that we added in `.bashrc` — that is, rm, cp, df, and ll.

Now, call the `current_directory_size()` function that we added in `.bashrc`:

```
$ cd ~ # cd to user's home directory
$ current_directory_size
Current directory is /home/foo with total used space 97G
$ cd /tmp
$  current_directory_size
Current directory is /tmp with total used space 48M
```

Make sure to move back the original `.bashrc` file whose backup we created at the beginning of this example, and source into it to get the settings reflected in the current shell session. This is required if you don't want any of the configuration changes that we did while playing out the preceding example:

```
$ mv ~/.bashrc.bak ~/.bashrc
$ source ~/.bashrc
```

 When bash is invoked as a non-login shell, it loads the configuration available in the `~/.bashrc`, `/etc/bashrc`, and `/etc/profile.d/*.sh` files.

.bash_profile

In a non-graphical system, after a successful login, the user gets a shell. Such a shell is called a login shell. When a bash is invoked as a login shell, first the `/etc/profile` file gets executed; this runs the script available in `/etc/profile.d/` as well. The following code snippet taken from `/etc/profile` also mentions this:

```
for i in /etc/profile.d/*.sh ; do
    if [ -r "$i" ]; then
        if [ "${-#*i}" != "$-" ]; then
            . "$i"
        else
```

These are global settings applied to any user's login shell. Furthermore, `~/.bash_profile` gets executed for a login shell. On a Fedora 22 system, the default content of the `~/.bash_profile` file looks as follows:

```
# .bash_profile

# Get the aliases and functions
if [ -f ~/.bashrc ]; then
        . ~/.bashrc
fi

# User specific environment and startup programs

PATH=$PATH:$HOME/.local/bin:$HOME/bin

export PATH
```

From the contents, we can see that it looks for the `.bashrc` file in a user's home directory. If the `.bashrc` file is available in a home directory, it gets executed. We also know that the `~/.bashrc` file executes the `/etc/bashrc` file as well. Next, we see that `.bash_profile` appends the `PATH` variable with the `$HOME/.local/bin` and `$HOME/bin` values. Furthermore, the modified `PATH` variable is exported as an environment variable.

A user can modify the `~/.bash_profile` file as per his/her customized configuration needs, such as default shell, editor for login shell, and so on.

The following example contains a modified configuration in `.bash_profile`. We will use `bash_profile` as its filename:

```
# .bash_profile

# Get the aliases and functions
if [ -f ~/.bashrc ]; then
        . ~/.bashrc
fi

# User specific environment and startup programs

PATH=$PATH:$HOME/.local/bin:$HOME/bin

export PATH

# Added configuration by us
# Setting user's default editor
EDITOR=/usr/bin/vim
# Show a welcome message to user with some useful information
echo "Welcome 'whoami'"
echo "You are using $SHELL as your shell"
echo "You are running 'uname ' release 'uname -r'"
echo "The machine architecture is 'uname -m'"
echo "$EDITOR will be used as default editor"
echo "Have a great time here!"
```

Changes are made after the **Added configuration by us** comment. Before we apply this new configuration to `~/.bash_profile`, we will first make a backup of the original file. This will help us in restoring the original content of the `.bash_profile` file:

```
$ cp ~/.bash_profile ~/.bash_profile.bak
```

A new file `.bash_profile.bak` will be created in the `home` directory. Now, we will copy our new configuration to `~/.bash_profile`:

```
$ cp bash_profile ~/.bash_profile
```

To see the reflected changes in a login shell, we can either login as a non-graphical interface or just perform `ssh` into the same machine to run a login shell. SSH (Secure Shell) is a cryptographic network protocol for initiating text-based shell sessions on remote machines in a secure way. In UNIX and Linux-based systems, SSH to a local or remote machine can be done using the `ssh` command. The `man` page of `ssh` (`man ssh`) shows all the capabilities provided by it. To do a remote login on the same machine, we can run `ssh username@localhost`:

```
$ ssh foo@localhost      #   foo is the username of user

    Last login: Sun Aug  2 20:47:46 2015 from 127.0.0.1
    Welcome foo
    You are using /bin/bash as your shell
    You are running Linux release 4.1.3-200.fc22.x86_64
    The machine architecture is x86_64
    /usr/bin/vim will be used as default editor
    Have a great time here!
```

We can see that all the details added by us are printed in a login shell. Another way to quickly test our new `.bash_profile` is by doing source to it:

```
$ source ~/.bash_profile

    Welcome foo
    You are using /bin/bash as your shell
    You are running Linux release 4.1.3-200.fc22.x86_64
    The machine architecture is x86_64
    /usr/bin/vim will be used as default editor
    Have a great time here!
```

To reset changes done in the `~/.bash_profile` file, copy from the `~/.bash_profile.bak` file that we created at the beginning of this example and source into it to get the changes reflected in the current shell:

```
$ mv ~/.bash_profile.bak ~/.bash_profile
$ source ~/.bash_profile
```

When bash is invoked as a login shell, it loads the configuration available in the `/etc/profile`, `/etc/profile.d/*.sh`, `~/.bash_profile`, `.~/.bashrc`, and `~/etc/bashrc` files.

.bash_logout

The `.bash_logout` file present in a user's home directory gets executed every time a login shell exits. This is useful when a user has logged in remotely or has a non-graphical interface. A user can add clean-up tasks to be performed before he/she logs off from a system. A clean-up task may include removing the temporary files created, clearing environment variables, logging off important data, archiving or encrypting certain tasks, uploading onto the Web, and so on.

Knowing your history

Shells provide an interesting feature that allows you to find out the history of all commands you have executed previously in a shell. It often happens that we forget what command was typed on the previous day to perform a task. We may or may not be able to recall the exact syntax, but it is very convenient that we can refer to the history saved by the shell.

Shell variables controlling the history

There are shell variables that can be altered to change what and how much history a user can see. These shell variables are mentioned in the following table:

Name	Value
HISTFILE	Name of file in which by default history will be saved
HISTFILESIZE	Number of commands to be kept in history file
HISTSIZE	Number of history to be stored in memory for current session
HISTCONTROL	A colon-separated list of values controlling how commands are saved on the history list

The value of the HISTCONTROL shell variable can be:

Value	Description
ignorespace	Lines which starts with a blank space, doesn't save in history list
ignoredups	Don't save lines which matches in previous saved history list
ignoreboth	Applies both ignorespace and ignoredups
erasedups	Remove all previous lines from history matching current line before saving it in history file

Let's see what values these shell variables may contain:

```
$   echo $HISTFILE
/home/foo/.bash_history
$ echo $HISTFILESIZE
1000
$ echo $HISTSIZE
1000
$ echo $HISTCONTROL
ignoredups
```

From the value obtained, we can see that the default history is saved into the .bash_history file of a user's home directory, with the maximum history command lines saved as 1000. Also, any duplicate history that is already present in the previous history line isn't saved.

The history builtin command

Shells provide the history builtin command so that a user will know the history of commands executed up to now.

Running the history without any options, prints all the previously typed commands on `stdout`. The sequence of commands are provided oldest to latest as we go from top to bottom of the output:

```
$ history  # Prints all commands typed previously on stdout

$ history | tail -n10    # Prints last 10 commands executed
```

```
726  vim bash_profile
727  cp bash_profile ~/.bash_profile
728  vim bash_profile
729  source bash_profile
730  man ssh
731  exit
732    source ~/.bash_profile
733  history
734  history |less
735  history | tail -n10
```

The following table explains the options available with the `history` shell built - in command:

Option	Description
-a	Append the new history lines into history immediately
-c	Clears history from current list
-d offset	Deletes history from offset specified
-r	Append the content of saved history to current list
-w	Write the current history list to the history file after overwriting existing saved history contents

To see the last five commands executed, we can also perform the following commands:

```
$ history 5
   769   cd /tmp/
   770   vi hello
   771   cd ~
   772   vi .bashrc
   773   history 5
```

We will find that all the commands executed match a given string from the history file. For example, search for commands having the set string in them:

```
$ history | grep set
  555   man setenv
  600   set | grep ENV_VAR2
  601   unset ENV_VAR2
  602   set | grep ENV_VAR2
  603   unset -u  ENV_VAR2
  604   set -u  ENV_VAR2
  605   set | grep ENV_VAR2
  737   set |grep HIST
  778   history | grep set
```

To clear all the history of commands saved and to append the history available in the current list, we can do the following (don't run the following commands if you don't want to loose the saved command history):

```
$ history -c  # Clears history from current list
$ history -w  # Overwrite history file and writes current list which is
empty
```

Modifying the default history behavior

By default, shell has some values set for managing the history. In the previous section, we saw that a maximum of 1000 lines of history will be stored in the history file. If a user spends most of his time working with a shell, he may have used 1000 or above commands in one or two days. In such a case, he will not be able to look at the history if he has typed a command ten days ago. Depending upon the individual use-case, a user can modify the number of lines to be stored in the history file.

Executing the following command will set the maximum number of lines the history file may have to 100000:

```
$ HISTFILESIZE=100000
```

Similarly, we can change where the history file should be saved. We saw that, by default, it is saved in the .bash_history file in the home directory. We can modify the HISTFILE shell variable and set it to whatever location we want our command history to be saved to:

```
$ HISTFILE=~/customized_history_path
```

Now the executed command history will be saved in the `customized_history_path` file in the home directory instead of the `~/.bash_history` file.

To make these changes reflect to all the shells being launched by a user and for all sessions, add these modifications to the `~/.bashrc` file.

Handy shortcuts for seeing the history

Depending upon a user's history size setting, the number of commands available in the history may be large. If a user wants to look for a specific command, he or she will have to look through the entire history, which can sometimes be troublesome. Shells provide some shortcuts to help us find a specific command previously executed. Knowledge of these shortcuts can save time in finding previously executed commands in the history.

[Ctrl + r]

While working in a shell, the *[Ctrl + r]* shortcut allows you to search for a command in the history. Start typing a command after pressing *[Ctrl + r]*; the shell shows a complete command that matches the substring of the command typed. To move forward to the next match, type *[Ctrl + r]* on the keyboard again and so on:

```
$ [ctrl + r]
(reverse-i-search)'his': man history
```

We can see that typing `his`, suggested from history `man history` that we previously typed.

Up and down arrow key

The up and down arrow keys available on the keyboard can be used to go back and forward in the history of commands previously executed by the user. For example, to get the previous command, press the up arrow key once. To go back even further, press the up arrow key again and so on. Further, to go forward in the history use the down arrow key.

!!

The shortcut ! ! can be used to reexecute the last command executed in the shell:

```
$ ls /home/
lost+found   foo
$ !!
ls /home/
lost+found   foo
```

!(search_string)

This shortcut executes the last command starting with `search_string`:

```
$ !l
ls /home/
lost+found   skumari
$ !his
history 12
```

!?(search_string)

This shortcut executes the last command found with the substring `search_string`:

```
$ !?h
ls /home/
lost+found   skumari
```

Task management

When an application runs, it is possible that it will run for a long period of time or run until the computer shuts down. While running an application in a shell, we know that a shell prompt only comes back when running a program in the shell completes successfully or terminates due to some error. Unless we get a shell prompt back, we can't run another command in the same shell. We can't even close that shell because it will close the running process.

Also, to run another application, we will have to open another shell in a new terminal and then run it. It can become difficult and tedious to manage if we have to run a lot of tasks. Shells provide ways to run a task in the background and suspend, kill, or move back in the foreground.

Running tasks in the background

A task can be started as a background in a shell by appending an ampersand (&).

For example, we want to search for a string in the entire filesystem. Depending upon the filesystem's size and the number of files, it may take a lot of time. We can call the grep command to search for a string and save the result in a file. A filesystem hierarchy in Linux starts from the root('/').

```
$ grep -R "search Text" / 2>/dev/null >  out1.txt &
[1] 8871
$
```

Here, the grep searches for a string in the entire filesystem, sends any error message to /dev/null, and saves the search result into the out1.txt file. An ampersand (&) at the end sends the entire job to the background, prints PID of the started task, and returns back the shell prompt.

Now, we can do other work in the same opened shell and perform other tasks.

Sending a running task to the background

It often happens that we run a task in a shell normally — that is, as a foreground task — but later we want to move it to the background. It is possible to do this by first suspending the current task using [*Ctrl + z*] and then using bg to move the task to the background.

Consider the last text search as an example. We start a search normally as follows:

```
$  grep -R "search Text" / 2>/dev/null >  out2.txt
```

We will not see anything happening on the shell and we will just keep waiting for a shell prompt to return. Alternatively, we can suspend the running job using [Ctrl + z]:

```
[ctrl + z]
[2]+  Stopped                 grep -R "search Text"  / 2> /dev/null > out2.txt
```

Then, to send a suspended task to continue running in the background, use the
bg command:

```
$ bg
[2]+ grep -R "search Text"  / 2> /dev/null > out2.txt
```

Listing background tasks

To find out which tasks are running in the background or suspended in the current
shell, jobs shell built - in is used as follows:

```
$ jobs

    [1]-  Running          grep -R "search Text" / 2> /dev/null > out1.txt &
    [2]+ Running           grep -R "search Text" / 2> /dev/null > out2.txt &
```

Here, index [1] and [2] are job numbers.

The character '+' identifies the job that would be used as a default by the fg or bg
command, and the character '-' identifies the job that would become a default if the
current default job exits or terminates.

Create another task and suspend it using the following commands:

```
$ grep -R "search Text" / 2>/dev/null >  out3.txt
    [ctrl + z]
    [3]+  Stopped          grep -R "search Text"  / 2> /dev/null > out3.txt
    $ jobs
    [1]      Running        grep -R "search Text" / 2> /dev/null > out1.txt &
    [2]-  Running           grep -R "search Text" / 2> /dev/null > out2.txt &
    [3]+ Stopped            grep-R "search Text" / 2> /dev/null > out3.txt
```

To view PID of all background and suspended tasks, we can use the –p option:

```
$ jobs -p

    8871
    8873
    8874
```

PID of jobs is in sequence. To view only the tasks running in the background, the -r option is used as follows:

```
$ jobs -r

   [1]    Running                    grep -R "search Text" / 2> /dev/null >
   out1.txt &
   [2]- Running                      grep -R "search Text" / 2> /dev/null >
   out2.txt &
```

To view only the suspended tasks, the -s option is used as follows:

```
$ jobs -s

   [3]+ Stopped                      grep-R "search Text" / 2> /dev/null >
   out3.txt
```

To view a particular index job, use an index number with the jobs command:

```
$ jobs 2

   [2]- Running                      grep -R "search Text" / 2> /dev/null >
   out2.txt &
```

Moving tasks to the foreground

We can move a background or suspended task to the foreground using the shell built - in command fg:

```
$ jobs  # Listing background and suspended tasks

   [1]    Running                    grep -R "search Text" / 2> /dev/null >
   out1.txt &
   [2]- Running                      grep -R "search Text" / 2> /dev/null >
   out2.txt &
   [3]+ Stopped                      grep-R "search Text" / 2> /dev/null >
   out3.txt
```

The character '+' is mentioned in the job index 3. This means, running the fg command will run the third job in the foreground:

```
$ fg
$ grep -R "search Text" / 2> /dev/null > out3.txt


[ctrl + z]

[3]+  Stopped                        grep -R "search Text" / 2> /dev/null >
out3.txt
```

The following command suspends the third task:

```
$ jobs
[1]    Running                 grep -R "search Text" / 2> /dev/null >
out1.txt &
[2]-   Running                 grep -R "search Text" / 2> /dev/null >
out2.txt &
[3]+ Stopped                   grep-R "search Text" / 2> /dev/null > out3.
txt
```

To move a particular job to the foreground, use `fg` with a task index number:

```
$  fg 1  # Moving first tasks to foreground
$ grep -R "search Text" / 2> /dev/null > out1.txt
[ctrl + z]
[1]+  Stopped                  grep -R "search Text" / 2> /dev/null > out1.txt
```

Terminating tasks

We can also delete a running or suspended task if it's no longer needed. This can be done by using the `disown` shell built - in command:

```
$ jobs  # List running or suspended tasks in current shell
   [1]+  Stopped       grep -R "search Text" / 2> /dev/null > out1.txt
   [2]   Running       grep -R "search Text" / 2> /dev/null > out2.txt &
   [3]-  Stopped       grep -R "search Text" / 2> /dev/null > out3.txt
```

Using `disown` without any option, deletes a task that has the character '+' mentioned with a task:

```
$ disown
   bash: warning: deleting stopped job 1 with process group 8871
$ jobs  # Listing available jobs
   [2]-  Running       grep -R "search Text" / 2> /dev/null > out2.txt &
   [3]+  Stopped       grep -R "search Text" / 2> /dev/null > out3.txt
```

To delete running tasks, the `-r` option is used:

```
$ disown -r
   jobs
   [3]-  Stopped                        grep -R "search Text" / 2> /dev/null >
   out3.txt
```

To remove all tasks, the `-a` option is used as follows:

```
$ disown -a  # Gives warning for deleting a suspended task

bash: warning: deleting stopped job 3 with process group 8874

$ jobs
```

The output of `jobs` shows nothing because all the suspended and running tasks got deleted by the `-a` option.

Summary

After reading this chapter, you now know how to create and modify environment variables in a shell. You also know how `.bashrc` and `.bash_profile` help in making changes that are available permanently for all sessions of a user. You learned how to search the history of commands that we have previously executed and also how to run and manage different tasks in a shell by using the `fg` and `bg` shell built - in commands.

In the next chapter, we will see what important types of files are available on Linux-based systems and what operations can be performed on them to get meaningful results.

6
Working with Files

For simplicity, everything in UNIX and Linux-based operating systems is treated as a file. Files in the filesystem are arranged in a hierarchical tree like a structure with the root of the tree denoted by '/' (forward slash). A node of the tree is either a directory or file where the directory is also a special type of file containing inode numbers and a corresponding filename entry of the list of files inside it. An inode number is an entry in an inode table that contains metadata information related to the file.

In this chapter, we will take a closer look at the important and commonly used file types. We will see how we can create, modify, and perform other useful operations on files. We will also see how to monitor a list of files opened by a process or user.

This chapter will cover the following topics in detail:

- Performing basic file operations
- Moving and copying files
- Comparing files
- Finding files
- Links to a file
- Special files
- Temporary files
- Permission and ownership
- Getting the list of open files
- Configuration files

Performing basic file operations

Most commonly used files are regular files and directories. In the following subsection, we will see the basic file operations.

Creating files

We can create both regular files and directories in shell using different shell commands.

Directory file

A directory is a special type of file that contains a list of filenames and a corresponding inode number. It acts as a container or folder to hold files and directories.

To create a new directory through shell, we can use the `mkdir` command:

```
$ mkdir dir1
```

We can also provide multiple directories' name as arguments to the `mkdir` command as follows:

```
$ mkdir dir2 dir3 dir4  # Creates multiple directories
```

We can create a parent directory if the specified pathname to `mkdir` is not present. This is done using the `-p` option in `mkdir`:

```
$ mkdir -p /tmp/dir1/dir2/dir3
```

Here, if `dir1` and `dir2` are the parent directories for `dir3` and don't exist already, the `-p` option will create the `dir1` directory first and then `dir2` subdirectory inside `dir1` and the `dir3` subdirectory inside `dir2`.

Regular file

In general, text and binary files are known as regular files. In shell, a regular file can be created in multiple ways. Some of them are mentioned in the following sections.

Touch command

A new regular file can also be created using the `touch` command. It is mainly used to modify the timestamp of the existing file, but if the file doesn't exist, a new file is created:

```
$ touch newfile.txt  # A new empty file newfile.txt gets created
$ test -f newfile.txt && echo File exists  # Check if file exists
File exists
```

Using the command line editors

We can open any command line editor; for example, `vi/vim`, emacs, nano in shell, write content, and save content in file.

Now, we will create and write a text using the `vi` editor:

```
$ vi foo.txt  # Opens vi editor to write content
```

Press the key *I* to enter the INSERT mode of vi and then type the text as shown in the following screenshot:

After writing the text, press the *Esc* key and then type the `:wq` command to save and exit from the vi editor. To know `vi/vim` in detail, refer to its `man` page or the online documentation (`http://www.vim.org/docs.php`):

Using the cat command

We can even use the `cat` command to write the content into an existing or a new regular file, as follows:

```
$ cat > newfile1.txt
We are using cat command
to create a new file and write into
it
[Ctrl + d]      # Press Ctrl + d to save and exit
$ cat newfile1.txt  # See content of file
We are using cat command
to create a new file and write into
it
```

By using the `>>` operator instead of `>`, we can append instead of overwriting the file's content.

Redirecting the command's output

While executing a command in bash or script, we can redirect results into an existing or a new file:

```
$ ls -l /home > newfile2.txt  #File gets created containing command
output
$ cat newfile2.txt
total 24
drwx------.    2    root    root    16384  Jun  11  00:46    lost+found
drwx-x---+ 41  foo     foo    4096   Aug  22  12:19    foo
```

Modifying files

To modify the content of a regular file in shell, open a file in an editor, make the required changes, and then save and exit. We can also use the `>>` operator to append the command's output to the specified file:

```
Command >> file.txt
```

For example, we will save the `ls` output of `/home` in the `ls_output.txt` file:

```
$ ls /home/ >> ls_output.txt
$ cat ls_output.txt  # Viewing content of file
lost+found
foo
```

Now, we will append the `ls` output of another directory `/home/foo/` as follows:

```
$ ls /home/foo >> ls_output.txt
lost+found
foo
Desktop
Documents
Downloads
Pictures
```

We saw that the `ls_output.txt` file gets modified by appending the content of the `ls` command output.

Viewing files

To view the content of a regular file, we can simply open a file in an editor such as vi/vim, emacs and nano. We can also use the `cat`, `less` and `more` commands to view the file's content.

To view the contents of a directory, we use the `ls` command:

```
$ ls /home/
lost+found  foo
```

To view the contents of a directory recursively, use `ls` with the `-R` or `--recursive` option.

Viewing content using cat

We can use the `cat` command to view the content of the file as follows:

```
$ cat newfile1.txt
We are using cat command
to create a new file and write into
it
$ cat -n newfile1.txt    # Display line number as well
     1  We are using cat command
     2  to create a new file and write into
     3  it
```

more and less

The more and less commands are very useful and handy to view a large file that doesn't fit on the current terminal.

The more command displays the content of a file in page format, in which we can scroll up and down to view the remaining contents of the file:

```
$ more /usr/share/dict/words
```

A file path is passed as an argument to the more command. In the above example, it will display the content of the file words available in the /usr/share/dict/ directory.

The key *s* is used to skip forward *k* lines of text. The key *f* is used to skip forward k screenful of text. The key *b* is used to skip backward k screenful of text.

The less command is more popular and widely used to view the content of large files. One of the advantages of using the less command is that it doesn't load entire files in the beginning and as a result, viewing the content of large files is faster.

The usage of less is very similar to the more command:

```
$ less   /usr/share/dict/words
```

Navigation is much easier while using the less command. It also has more options to customize the filtered view of a file's content.

The more and less commands can take an input from stdin if no input file is provided. Use a pipe ('|') to give an input from stdin:

```
$ cat /usr/share/dict/words | more     # cat output redirected to more
$ grep ^.{3}$ /usr/share/dict/words | less  # Matches all 3 character
words
```

See the man page of more and less for the detailed usage.

 The behavior of the more command may vary on different systems because of its different implementations.

Deleting files

We can also delete regular files and directories if they are no longer required.

Deleting a regular file

To delete a regular file, we use the rm command in shell.

The rm command deletes the file if it exists, otherwise it prints an error on stdout if it doesn't exist:

```
$ rm newfile1.txt     # Deletes if file exists
$ rm newfile1.txt     # Prints error message if file doesn't exist
rm: cannot remove 'newfile1.txt': No such file or directory
```

To ignore an error message, rm can be used with the -f option:

```
$ rm -f newfile1.txt
$ rm -i  newfile.txt   # Interactive deletion of file
rm: remove regular empty file 'newfile.txt'?
```

Enter the key *y* to delete a file and *n* to skip the deletion of a file.

Deleting a directory

To delete a directory, we can use the rmdir and rm commands. We will consider directories that are created in the Directory files under the File creation subtopic:

```
$ rmdir dir2/  # Deletes directory dir2
$ rmdir dir1/  #  Fails to delete because of non-empty directory
rmdir: failed to remove 'dir1/': Directory not empty
```

To delete a nonempty directory, first delete the contents and then remove the directory. We can also use rm to remove an empty or a nonempty directory.

The -d option removes an empty directory as follows:

```
$ ls dir3/  # Directory dir3 is empty
$ rm -d dir3/  # Empty diretcory dir3 gets deleted
$ ls dir1/  # Diretcory dir1 is not empty
dir2
$ rm -d dir1/  # Fails to delete non-empty directory dir1
rm: cannot remove 'dir1': Directory not empty
```

The option -r, -R, or --recursive removes the directory and its contents recursively:

```
$ rm -ri dir1/  # Asks to remove directory dir1 recursively
rm: descend into directory 'dir1'?  Y
```

Typing *y* confirms that dir1 should be deleted.

> Use rm carefully with the -r option. If possible, use it with the -i option to avoid an accidental deletion of an entire directory's contents.

Moving and copying files

We often need to copy or move files from one location to another in order to arrange files according to the need. We also can copy our computer data to an external drive or another computer available locally or remotely in order to keep the backup of the important data.

Moving files

Moving regular files and directories is useful when we want to keep exactly one copy of the data at a new location. The mv command is used to move files from one location to another.

The syntax of using the mv command is as follows:

```
mv [option] source... destination
```

Here, source is the file or directory to be moved. Multiple source files can be specified and destination is the location in which the files and directories should be moved.

Some of the important options of the mv command are explained in following table:

Option	Description
-n	Don't overwrite an existing file
-i	Prompt before overwriting an existing file
-f	Don't prompt while overwriting an existing file
-u	Move a source file only when the source is newer than the destination or when the destination is missing
v	Print name of the files being moved

Moving a directory to a new location

To move a directory from one location to another, execute the following command:

```
$ mkdir ~/test_dir1  # Directory test_dir1 created in home directory
$ mv ~/test_dir1/ /tmp # moving directory to /tmp
```

The test_dir1 directory has been moved to /tmp and no copy of test_dir1 exists in the home directory now.

Now, we will create a directory called test_dir1 again in the user's home directory:

```
$ mkdir ~/test_dir1  # Directory test_dir1 created in home directory
```

Try again to move test_dir1 in /tmp with the -i option:

```
$ mv -i ~/test_dir1/ /tmp
mv: overwrite '/tmp/test_dir1'?
```

We can see that the -i option asks a user explicitly whether we want to overwrite an existing directory with a new directory or not.

 Use the mv command with the -i option to avoid an accidental overwrite of a file.

Renaming a file

We can also use the mv command to rename a filename. For example, we have the test_dir1 directory in the /tmp directory. Now, we want to rename it as test_dir. We can execute the following command:

```
$ mv  /tmp/test_dir1/  /tmp/test_dir  # directory got renamed to test_dir
```

Copying files

Creating copies of files is a very common operation that can be performed locally or to a remote system.

Copying files locally

To copy the files on a local machine, the cp command is used.

The syntax of using the cp command is as follows:

```
cp [option] source ... destination
```

Here, source can be a single file, multiple file, or a directory, while destination can be a file if source is a single file. Otherwise, destination will be a directory.

Some of important options to the cp command are as follows:

Options	Description
-f	Don't prompt while overwriting an existing file
-i	Prompt before overwriting an existing file
-R	Copy directories recursively
-u	Copy a source file only when the source is newer than the destination or when the destination is missing
-p	Preserve attributes of a copied file with the original file
-v	Verbose output of which file is being copied

Copying a file to another location

To copy a file to another location, execute the following command:

```
$ touch ~/copy_file.txt     # Creating a file
$ cp ~/copy_file.txt /tmp/  # Copying file to /tmp
```

Now, we have two copies of the copy_file.txt file that are at the user's home directory and the /tmp directory.

To copy a directory, we use cp with the -R option:

```
$ mkdir ~/test_dir2  # Creating a test diretcory
$ cp -R ~/test_dir2 /tmp/
```

The test_dir2 directory gets copied to /tmp along with all the contents available in the directory.

Copying files remotely

To copy files on a remote machine, the scp command is used. It copies files between hosts on a network. The scp command uses ssh to authenticate the target host and transfer data.

The simple syntax of scp is as follows:

```
scp [option] user1@host1:source user2@host2:destination
```

Here, in `user1@host1:source`, `user1` is the username of the source from where a file will be copied and `host1` is the hostname or IP address; `source` can be a file or a directory to be copied.

In `user2@host2:destination`, `user2` is the username of the target host where files should be copied and `host2` is the hostname or IP address; `destination` can be a file or directory where it gets copied. If no destination is specified, a copy will be made in the target host's home directory.

If no remote source and destination to provided, a copy will be made locally.

A few important options of `scp` are discussed in the following table:

Option	Description
`-C`	Enable compression while transferring data over a network
`-l limit`	Limit the used bandwidth specified in Kbit/s
`-p`	Preserve attributes of a copied file with the original file
`-q`	Don't print any progress output on `stdout`
`-r`	Copy directory recursively
`-v`	Verbose output while the copy is in progress

Copying files to a remote server

To copy files to a remote server, it is very important that the `ssh` server is already running on the server. If it is not, make sure to start the `ssh` server. To copy files, use the `scp` command as follows:

```
$ scp -r ~/test_dir2/ foo@localhost:/tmp/test_dir2/
```

Here, we have made a copy to a local machine. So, the hostname used is `localhost`. Now, we have another directory `test_dir2` inside `/tmp/test_dir2/`:

```
$ ls -l /tmp/test_dir2
total 0
drwxrwxr-x. 2 foo foo 40 Aug 25 00:44 test_dir2
```

Comparing files

A comparison between two similar files makes sense in order to know what differences exist between the two files. For example, comparing the results obtained by a command ran on two sets of data. Another example can be comparing an older and a newer version of a shell script file in order to know what modifications have been made in script. Shell provides the `diff` command for file comparison.

Files comparison using diff

The `diff` command is used to compare files line by line. The syntax of using the `diff` command is as follows:

```
diff [option] file1 file2
```

Where, `file1` and `file2` are the files to be compared.

The options of the `diff` command are explained in the following table:

Option	Description
`-q`	Only print if files differ
`-s`	Print a message on `stdout` if the two files are identical
`-y`	Display the `diff` results side by side
`-i`	Do case-insensitive comparison of the files' content
`-b`	Ignore changes in the number of whitespace
`-u NUM`	Output NUM (default 3) lines of unified context
`-a`	Consider files as text files while comparison

Example

The `diff` command shows the comparison results for the added, removed, and modified lines between two files.

We will consider the `comparison_file1.txt` and `comparison_file2.txt` text files as an example:

```
$ cat comparison_file1.txt # Viewing content of file
    This is a comparison example.

    This line should be removed.
    We have added multiple consecutive blank spaces.
    THIS line CONTAINS both CAPITAL and small letters
$ cat comparison_file2.txt # Viewing content of file
    This is a comparison example.
    We have added        multiple consecutive blank spaces.
    this line contains both CAPITAL and small letters
    Addition of a line
```

Now, we will compare the `comparison_file1.txt` and `comparison_file2.txt` files:

```
$ diff  comparison_file1.txt  comparison_file2.txt
    2,5c2,4
    <
    < This line should be removed.
    < We have added multiple consecutive blank spaces.
    < THIS line CONTAINS both CAPITAL and small letters
    ---
    > We have added      multiple consecutive blank spaces.
    > this line contains both CAPITAL and small letters
    > Addition of a line
```

Here, < (less than) means removed lines and > (greater than) means added lines.

Using the `-u` option makes the `diff` output even more readable as follows:

```
$ diff -u comparison_file1.txt comparison_file2.txt
    --- comparison_file1.txt      2015-08-23 16:47:28.360766660 +0530
    +++ comparison_file2.txt      2015-08-23 16:40:01.629441762 +0530
    @@ -1,6 +1,5 @@
     This is a comparison example.
     -
    -This line should be removed.
    -We have added multiple consecutive blank spaces.
    -THIS line CONTAINS both CAPITAL and small letters
    +We have added      multiple consecutive blank spaces.
    +this line contains both CAPITAL and small letters
    +Addition of a line
```

Here, '-' tells the lines available in an older file (`comparison_file1.txt`), but which is no longer present in the newer file (`comparison_file2.txt`).

The '+' tells lines being added in newer file (`comparison_file2.txt`).

We can even do a case-insensitive comparison of the content using the -i option:

```
$ diff -i comparison_file1.txt comparison_file2.txt
    2,4c2
    <
    < This line should be removed.
    < We have added multiple consecutive blank spaces.
    ---
    > We have added        multiple consecutive blank spaces.
    5a4
    > Addition of a line
```

To ignore multiple blank spaces, use diff with make -b option:

```
$ diff -bi  comparison_file1.txt  comparison_file2.txt
    2,3d1
    <
    < This line should be removed.
    5a4
    > Addition of a line
```

Finding files

In a filesystem, there is huge number of files available. Sometimes, there are external devices that are attached as well, which may also contain huge number of files. Imagine that there are millions and billions of files in a system and in which we have to search for a specific file or pattern of a file. Manual searching of a file is possible if the number of files is from 10 to 100, but it is almost impossible to search in millions of files. To solve this problem, UNIX and Linux provide the find command. It is a very useful command for searching files in a computer.

The syntax of using the find command is as follows:

```
find search_path [option]
```

Here, in search_path, specify the path in which find should search for file_search_pattern.

A few important options are mentioned in the following table:

Option	Description
-P	Don't follow symbolic link. This is default behavior
-L	Follow symbolic link while searching
-exec cmd ;	Execute command cmd passed as parameter to -exec
-mount	Don't search in other file system
-executable	Matches executable files
-group gname	File belongs to group gname
-user uname	Files owned by user uname
-name pattern	Search file for given pattern
-iname pattern	Case insensitive search of file for given pattern
-inum N	Search file with inode number N
-samefile name	File with same inode number as name
-regex pattern	Match files with given regular expression pattern. Matches for whole path.
-iregex pattern	Case insensitive match of files with given regular expression pattern. Matches for whole path.

Searching files according to use case

The following shell script shows some use cases of how to use the find command:

```bash
#!/bin/bash
# Filename: finding_files.sh
# Description: Searching different types of file in system

echo -n "Number of C/C++ header files in system: "
find / -name "*.h" 2>/dev/null |wc -l
echo -n "Number of shell script files in system: "
find / -name "*.sh" 2>/dev/null |wc -l
echo "Files owned by user who is running the script ..."
echo -n "Number of files owned by user $USER :"
find / -user $USER 2>/dev/null |wc -l
echo -n "Number of executable files in system: "
find / -executable 2>/dev/null | wc -l
```

The following is the sample output after executing the preceding `finding_files.sh` script:

```
Number of C/C++ header files in system: 73950
Number of shell script files in system: 2023
Files owned by user who is running the script ...
Number of files owned by user foo :341726
Number of executable files in system: 127602
```

Finding and deleting a file based on inode number

The `find` command can be used to find a file based on its inode number.

```
$ find ~/ -inum 8142358
/home/foo/Documents
```

The `-inum` option is good to use with `exec` to delete files that cannot be deleted by a filename. For example, a file named `-test.txt` can't be deleted using the `rm` command:

```
$ ls -i ~ |grep  test  # Viewing file with its inode number
8159146 -test.txt
```

To delete the `-test.txt` file, execute the following command:

```
$ find ~/ -inum 8159146 -exec rm -i {} \;  # Interactive deletion
rm: remove regular file '/home/skumari/-test.txt?' y
```

Links to a file

A link to a file means referring the same file by different filenames. In Linux and Unix-based system, the following two types of links exist:

- A soft link or a symbolic link
- A hard link

To create links between files, the `ln` command can be used. The syntax is as follows:

```
ln [option] target link_name
```

Here, `target` is the filename for which a link has to be created and `link_name` is the name by which a link has to be created.

Soft link

A soft link is a special kind of file that just points to another file. This makes it easier to create a shortcut of a file and easy accessibility of a file to a different location in a filesystem.

To create a symbolic link of a file, the `ln` command is used with the `-s` option. For example, we will create a symbolic link of the `/tmp` directory in our home directory:

```
$ ln -s /tmp ~/local_tmp
```

Now, we have a symbolic link of the `/tmp` directory in our home directory by the name `local_tmp`. To access the `/tmp` data, we can also `cd` into the `~/local_tmp` directory. To know whether a file is a symbolic link or not, run `ls -l` on a file:

```
$ ls -l ~/local_tmp
lrwxrwxrwx. 1 foo foo 5 Aug 23 23:31 /home/foo/local_tmp -> /tmp/
```

If the first character of the first column is `l`, then it means it is a symbolic link. Also the last column says `/home/foo/local_tmp -> /tmp/`, which means `local_tmp` is pointing to `/tmp`.

Hard link

A hard link is a way to refer a file with different names. All such files will have the same inode number. An inode number is an index number in an inode table that contains metadata about a file.

To create a hard link of a file, use the `ln` command without any option. In our case, we will first create a regular file called `file.txt`:

```
$ touch file.txt
$ ls -l file.txt
-rw-rw-r--. 1 foo foo 0 Aug 24 00:13 file.txt
```

The second column of `ls` tells the link count. We can see that currently it is `1`.

Now, to create a hard link of `file.txt`, we will use the `ln` command:

```
$ ln file.txt hard_link_file.txt
```

To check whether a hard link is created for `file.txt`, we will see its link count:

```
$ ls -l file.txt
-rw-rw-r--. 2 foo foo 0 Aug 24 00:13 file.txt
```

Now, the link count is 2 because a hard link has been created with the name `hard_link_file.txt`.

We can also see that the inode number of the `file.txt` and `hard_link_file.txt` files are the same:

```
$ ls -i file.txt hard_link_file.txt
96844    file.txt
96844    hard_link_file.txt
```

Difference between hard link and soft link

The following table shows a few important differences between a hard link and a soft link:

Soft link	Hard link
The inode number of the actual file and the soft link file are different.	The inode number of the actual file and the hard link file are the same.
A soft link can be created across different filesystems.	A hard link can only be created in the same filesystem.
A soft link can link to both regular files and directories.	A hard link doesn't link to directories.
Soft links are not updated if the actual file is deleted. It keeps pointing to a nonexistent file.	Hard links are always updated if the actual file is moved or deleted.

Special files

The files other than regular files, directories, and link files are special files. They are as follows:

- The block device file
- The character device file
- The named pipe file
- The socket file

The block device file

A block device file is a file that reads and writes data in block. Such files are useful when data needs to be written in bulk. Devices such as hard disk drive, USB drive, and CD-ROM are considered as block device files. Data is written asynchronously and, hence, other users are not blocked to perform the write operation at the same time.

To create a block device file, mknod is used with the option b along with providing a major and minor number. A major number selects which device driver is being called to perform the input and output operation. A minor number is used to identify subdevices:

```
$ sudo mknod  block_device b 0X7 0X6
```

Here, 0X7 is a major number and 0X6 is a minor number in hexadecimal format:

```
$ ls -l block_device
brw-r--r--. 1 root root 7, 6 Aug 24 12:21 block_device
```

The first character of the first column is b, which means it is a block device file.

The fifth column of the ls output is 7 and 6. Here, 7 is a major number and 6 is a minor number in decimal format.

A character device file is a file that reads and writes data in character-by-character fashion. Such devices are synchronous and only one user can do the write operation at a time. Devices such as keyboard, printer, and mouse are known as character device files.

Following command will create a character special file:

```
$ sudo  mknod  character_device  c 0X78 0X60
```

Here, 0X78 is a major number and 0X60 is a minor number that is in hexadecimal format.

```
$ ls -l character_device  # viewing attribute of  character_device file
crw-r--r--. 1 root root 120, 96 Aug 24 12:21 character_device
```

The first character of the first column is c, which means it is a character device file. The fifth column of the ls output is 120 and 96. Here, 120 is a major number and 96 is a minor number in decimal format.

Named pipe file

Named pipe files are used by different system processes to communicate with each other. Such communication is also known as interprocess communication.

To create such a file, we use the `mkfifo` command:

```
$ mkfifo pipe_file      # Pipe file created
$ ls pipe_file          # Viewing file content
prw-rw-r--. 1 foo foo 0 Aug 24 01:41 pipe_file
```

Here, the first character of the first column is 'p', which means it is a pipe file. There are a lot of pipe files available in the `/dev` directory.

We can also create a named pipe using the `mknod` command with the `p` option:

```
$ mknod   named_pipe_file p
$ ls -l   named_pipe_file
prw-rw-r--. 1 foo foo 0 Aug 24 12:33 named_pipe_file
```

The following shell script demonstrates a reading message from a named pipe. The `send.sh` script creates a named pipe called `named_pipe`, if it doesn't exist, and then sends a message on it:

```
#!/bin/bash
# Filename: send.sh
# Description: Script which sends message over pipe

pipe=/tmp/named_pipe

if [[ ! -p $pipe ]]
then
  mkfifo $pipe
fi

echo "Hello message from Sender">$pipe
```

The `receive.sh` script checks whether a named pipe with the name `named_pipe` exists, reads a message from a pipe, and displays on `stdout`:

```
#!/bin/bash
#Filename: receive.sh
# Description: Script receiving message from sender from pipe file

pipe=/tmp/named_pipe

if [[ ! -p $pipe ]]
then
  echo "Reader is not running"
fi

while read line
do
  echo "Message from Sender:"
  echo $line
done < $pipe
```

To execute it, run `send.sh` in a terminal and `receive.sh` in another terminal:

```
$ sh send.sh  # In first terminal
$ sh receive.sh  # In second terminal
Message from Sender:
Hello message from Sender
```

Socket file

A socket file is used to pass information from one application to another. For example, if **Common UNIX Printing System (CUPS)** daemon is running and my printing application wants to communicate with it, then my printing application will write a request to a socket file where CUPS daemon is listening for upcoming requests. Once a request is written to a socket file, the daemon will serve the request:

```
$ ls -l /run/cups/cups.sock  # Viewing socket file attributes
srw-rw-rw-. 1 root root 0 Aug 23 15:39 /run/cups/cups.sock
```

The first character in the first column is `s`, which means it is a socket file.

Temporary files

Temporary files are the files that are needed for a short interval of time while an application is running. Such files are being used to keep intermediate results of running a program and they are no longer needed after the program execution is complete. In shell, we can create temporary files using the `mktemp` command.

Creating a temporary file using mktemp

The `mktemp` command creates a temporary file and prints its name on `stdout`. Temporary files are created by default in the `/tmp` directory.

The syntax of creating a temporary file is as follows:

```
$ mktmp
/tmp/tmp.xEXXxYeRcF
```

A file with the name `tmp.xEXXxYeRcF` gets created into the `/tmp` directory. We can further read and write into this file in an application for temporary use. Using the `mktemp` command instead of using a random name for a temporary filename avoids accidental overwrite of an existing temporary file.

To create a temporary directory, we can use the `-d` option with `mktemp`:

```
$ temp_dir=mktemp -d
$ echo $temp_dir
/tmp/tmp.Y6WMZrkcj4
```

Furthermore, we can explicitly delete it as well:

```
$ rm -r /tmp/tmp.Y6WMZrkcj4
```

We can even specify a template to use for a temporary file by providing an argument as `name.XXXX`. Here, `name` can be any name by which a temporary file should begin, and `XXXX` tells the length of a random character to be used after a dot (.). In general, while writing an application if temporary files are needed, the application name is given as the temporary file name.

For example, a test application needs to create a temporary file. To create a temporary file, we will use the following command:

```
$ mktemp test.XXXXX
test.q2GEI
```

We can see that the temporary file name begins with `test` and contains exactly five random letters.

 The time when temporary files will be cleaned up is distribution-specific.

Permission and ownership

As a user of a system, to access a file in Linux and UNIX, it is important that a user has the required permission for that specific file or directory. For example, as a regular user, perform `cd` into `/root`:

```
$ cd /root
bash: cd: /root/: Permission denied
```

We were not able to do so because of the permission denied error:

```
$ cd ~/
```

We were successfully able to do `cd` into the user's home directory because a user had the permission to access its own home directory.

Every file in UNIX or Linux has an owner and an associated group. It also has a set of permissions (read, write, and execute) with respect to the user, group, and others.

Viewing the ownership and permission of files

The `ls` command with the `-l` option is used to view the ownership and permission of a file:

```
$ touch permission_test_file.txt     #  Creating a file
$ ls -l  permission_test_file.txt     # Seeing files' attributes
-rw-rw-r-- 1 foo foo 0 Aug 24 16:59 permission_test_file.txt
```

Here, the first column of `ls` contains the permission information—that is, `-rw-rw-r--`.

The first character specifies a file's type, which is dash (-) in this example. A dash means that it is a regular file. It can have other characters as follows:

- p: This means it is a named pipe file
- d: This means it is a directory file
- s: This means it is a socket file
- c: This means it is a character device file
- b: This means it is a block device file

The next three characters belong to a user's or owner's permission. It can be either `rwx` or `dash` at any of these spaces. The permission `r` specifies that the read permission is available, `w` specifies that the write permission is available, and `x` specifies that the execute permission is available over the given file. If a dash is present, then the corresponding permission is missing. In the above example, an owner's permission is `rw-`, which means the owner has read and write permission on the `permission_test_file.txt` file but no execute permission.

The next three characters belong to a group's permission. It can be `rwx` or `dash` at any of these places if the corresponding permission is missing. In the preceding example, the permission given to a group is `rw-`, which means the read and write permissions are present and the execute permission is missing.

The next three characters belong to other's permission. In the preceding example, the permission given to others is `r--`, which means other users can read the content of the `permission_test_file.txt` file but can't modify or execute it.

The next column in the `ls -l` output—that is, the second column specifies who the owner of file is. In our example, the second column value is `foo`, which means `foo` has the ownership of the file. By default, the ownership of a file is given to whoever has created that file.

The third column in the `ls -l` output that specifies the group to which a file belongs to. In our case, the group of the `permission_test_file.txt` file is `foo`.

Changing permission

To change the permission of a file, the chmod command is used. The syntax of using chmod is as follows:

```
chmod [option] mode[,mode] file
```

Or,

```
chmod [option] octal-mode file
```

An important option of chmod is -R, which means change the files and directories permission recursively.

The mode can be [ugoa] [-+] [rwx].

Here, u is the owner, g is the group, o is other, and a is all users — that is, ugo.

Specifying - (minus) removes the specified permission and specifying + (plus) adds the specified permission.

The letters r(read), w(write), and x(execute) specify permissions.

The octal-mode specifies the rwx permission of a user together in octal format, which can be from 0 to 7. The following table explains the octal representation of a permission to a specific user:

Octal Value	Binary representation	Meaning
0	000	No read, write, and execute permissions (---)
1	001	Only execute permission (--x)
2	010	Only write permission (-w-)
3	011	Write and execute permissions (-wx)
4	100	Only read permission (r--)
5	101	Read and execute permissions (r-x)
6	110	Read and write permissions (rw-)
7	111	Read, write, and execute permissions (rwx)

To demonstrate the changing permission on a file, we will create a file as follows:

```
$ touch test_file.txt
$ ls -l test_file.txt    # Checking permission of file
-rw-rw-r--. 1 foo foo 0 Aug 24 18:59 test_file.txt
```

The default permission given to a regular file is the Read permission to an owner, group, and other. The Write permission is given to the owner and group. No execute permission is given to anyone.

Now, we want to modify a permission in such a way that only the owner can have the write permission, and keeping the other permission as it is. We can do this in the following way:

```
$ chmod 644 test_file.txt
$ ls -l tst_file.txt
-rw-r--r--. 1 foo foo 0 Aug 24 19:03 test_file.txt
```

Now, we can see that only an owner can modify test_file. While using octal mode, we have to specify the exact permission that we want to see further. In chmod, we gave octal_mode as 644; here the first octal digit, that is, 6 signifies the read, write, and execute permissions of the owner. Similarly, the second octal digit 4 specifies the permissions for the group and the third digit specifies the permission for others.

There is another way to modify a permission, which is by using mode. Mode is specified as [ugoa] [-+] [rwx]. Here, we only have to specify which permission we want to add or remove.

For example, we want to remove the write permission from an owner and add the execute permission to all. We can do this as follows:

```
$ chmod u-w,a+x test_file.txt
$ ls -l test_file.txt
-r-xr-xr-x. 1 foo foo 0 Aug 24 19:03 test_file.txt
```

Changing the owner and group

We can also change the owner and group ownership of a file. This allows flexibility to further modify the group and owner of a file.

Changing a file's owner

To change the owner of a command, chown is used. This is useful for sysadmin in different cases. For example, a user is working on a project and now the user is going to discontinue working on that project. In such a case, sysadmin can modify the ownership to a new user who is responsible for continuing that project. Sysadmin can change the ownership of a file to a new user for all the related files in a project.

In our previous example, `foo` is the owner of the `test_file.txt` file. Now, we want to transfer the ownership of a file to user `bar`.

If the user `bar` doesn't exist in a system, a new user bar can be created using the `useradd` command. The `useradd` command needs the root access.

Following command will create a new user called `bar`:

```
$ sudo useradd bar   # New user bar will be created
```

We can change ownership of `test_file.txt` file to user `bar` by executing the following command as `root` or `sudo`:

```
$ sudo chown bar test_file.txt   # Changing ownership of file to user bar
$ ls -l  test_file.txt
-r-xr-xr-x. 1 bar foo 0 Aug 24 19:03 test_file.txt
```

We can see that the ownership of a file is changed to bar.

Changing group ownership

To modify the group ownership of a file, we can either use the `chown` or `chgrp` command. To create a new group, the `groupadd` command is used as `sudo` or `root`. For example, we want to create a new group called `test_group`:

```
$ sudo groupadd test_group
```

Now, we will change the group of the example file `test_file.txt` by using the `chown` command. This can be done by executing the following command:

```
$ sudo chown :test_group test_file.txt  # Modifying group ownership
$ ls -l test_file.txt
-r-xr-xr-x. 1 bar test_group 0 Aug 24 19:03 test_file.txt
```

We can see that the group has been modified to `test_group`. To change the group using the `chgrp` command, we can execute the following command:

```
$  sudo chgrp bar test_file.txt  # Changing group ownership to bar
$ ls -l test_file.txt
-r-xr-xr-x. 1 bar bar 0 Aug 24 19:03 test_file.txt
```

Now, we will revert back the owner and group to `foo` for the `test_file.txt` file:

```
$ sudo chown foo:foo test_file.txt
$ ls -l test_file.txt
-r-xr-xr-x. 1 foo foo 0 Aug 24 19:03 test_file.txt
```

The new owner name is provided before : (colon) and the group name after : ,while modifying the owner and group ownership using the `chown` command.

Getting the list of open files

We know that there can be millions of files available in a system, which can be binary files, text files, directories, and so on. When a file is not in use, they are just available on a storage device as `0 and 1`. To view or process a file, it needs to be opened. An application that is executing may open multiple files. Knowing what files are opened by a running application is very useful. To know the list of opened files, the `lsof` command is used.

Executing the following command gives the list of all opened files:

```
$ lsof
```

This gives a huge output of all the opened files.

Knowing the files opened by a specific application

To know the list of files opened by a specific application, first get the **Process ID** (**PID**) of the running application:

```
$ pidof application_name
```

For example, let's run `cat` without any parameter:

```
$ cat
```

In another terminal, run the following commands:

```
$ pidof cat
15913
$ lsof -p 15913
```

Alternatively, we can directly write the following command:

```
$ lsof -p 'pidof cat'
```

The following is a sample screenshot of the `lsof` output:

```
lsof: WARNING: can't stat() tracefs file system /sys/kernel/debug/tracing
      Output information may be incomplete.
COMMAND   PID     USER   FD   TYPE DEVICE  SIZE/OFF    NODE NAME
cat     15946 skumari  cwd    DIR   0,37      1020   11831 /tmp
cat     15946 skumari  rtd    DIR    8,1      4096       2 /
cat     15946 skumari  txt    REG    8,1     54128 1442296 /usr/bin/cat
cat     15946 skumari  mem    REG    8,1 107714000 1448050 /usr/lib/locale/locale-archive
cat     15946 skumari  mem    REG    8,1   2095280 1448004 /usr/lib64/libc-2.21.so
cat     15946 skumari  mem    REG    8,1    158816 1447997 /usr/lib64/ld-2.21.so
cat     15946 skumari   0u    CHR  136,2       0t0       5 /dev/pts/2
cat     15946 skumari   1u    CHR  136,2       0t0       5 /dev/pts/2
cat     15946 skumari   2u    CHR  136,2       0t0       5 /dev/pts/2
```

In the output, we see that there are various columns of results. The first column is COMMAND — that is, for the application this file has been opened, the PID column specifies the PID with which the file has been opened, USER tells which user has opened the file, FD is the file descriptor, TYPE specifies the type of file, DEVICE specifies the device number with values separated by a comma, SIZE/OFF specifies the size of the file or the file offset in bytes, and NAME is the filename with the absolute path.

In the output, we can see that the application has opened `cat` binary from `/usr/bin`. It has also loaded the shared library files such as `libc-2.21.so` and `ld-2.21.so` available in `/usr/lib64/`. Also, there is a character device `dev/pts/2` that has been opened.

Listing the applications that opened a file

We can also find out which all applications opened a file. This can be done by executing the following command:

```
$ lsof /usr/bin/bash
```

The following is the sample output:

```
COMMAND    PID     USER  FD   TYPE DEVICE SIZE/OFF    NODE NAME
startkde  1348 skumari txt    REG    8,1  1071960 1447000 /usr/bin/bash
bash      1721 skumari txt    REG    8,1  1071960 1447000 /usr/bin/bash
sh        9524 skumari txt    REG    8,1  1071960 1447000 /usr/bin/bash
bash      9613 skumari txt    REG    8,1  1071960 1447000 /usr/bin/bash
bash     11202 skumari txt    REG    8,1  1071960 1447000 /usr/bin/bash
bash     15947 skumari txt    REG    8,1  1071960 1447000 /usr/bin/bash
```

From the output, we can see that the `bash` file has been opened by six running applications.

Knowing the files opened by a user

To know the list of files opened by a specific user, run `lsof` with the `-u` option. The syntax is as follows:

```
lsof -u user_name
```

For example, consider the following command:

```
$ lsof -u foo | wc -l
525
```

This means, currently `525` files are opened by the user root.

Configuration files

Configuration or config files are regular files that contain settings for an application. During the initial stage of execution, many applications in Linux and UNIX read settings from config file(s) and configure the application accordingly.

Viewing and modifying configuration files

Configuration files are generally present in the `/etc/` directory and can be viewed using the `cat` command.

For example, consider viewing the `resolv.conf` config file:

```
$ cat /etc/resolv.conf
    # Generated by NetworkManager
    search WirelessAP
    nameserver 192.168.1.1
```

The `resolv.conf` file contains the order in which to contact DNS servers.

We can also modify a configuration file to meet our requirements. For example, we can add another DNS entry in the `/etc/resolv.conf` file with the DNS value `8.8.8.8`, if some of network URLs are accessible via `192.168.1.1`. The modified `cat /etc/resolv.conf` will look like the following:

```
$ cat /etc/resolv.conf
    # Generated by NetworkManager
    search WirelessAP
    nameserver 192.168.1.1
    nameserver 8.8.8.8
```

There are a lot of other config files available in a system such as `ssh`, `passwd`, `profile`, `sysconfig`, `crontab`, `inittab`, and so on, in the `/etc/` directory.

Summary

After reading this chapter, you should now know that the UNIX and Linux-based operating system treats everything as files that can be further categorized as regular, directory, link, block device, character device, socket, and pipe files. You should also know how to perform basic operations on any of these files. Now, you should have good knowledge of how to view and modify the permissions and ownership of a file. You should also know how to monitor and manage the list of open files in a system using the `lsof` command.

In the next chapter, you will learn how a process gets created in a system and how to monitor and manage all running processes. We will also see how two or more processes communicate with each other using **Inter Process Communication (IPC)** mechanism.

7
Welcome to the Processes

A program under execution is known as **process**. When an operating system gets booted up, multiple processes get started in order to provide various functionalities and user interfaces so that a user can easily perform the required tasks. For example, when we start a command line server, we will see a terminal with bash or any other shell process that has been started.

In Linux, we have full control over processes. It allows us to create, stop, and kill processes. In this chapter, we will see how a process is created and managed by using commands such as top, ps, and kill and by changing its scheduling priority. We will also see how a signal can lead to the sudden termination of a process and also the ways to handle signals in a script using the command trap. We will also see one of the beautiful features of processes called Inter-process communication, which allows them to communicate with each other.

This chapter will cover the following topics in detail:

- Process management
- Listing and monitoring processes
- Process substitution
- Process scheduling priorities
- Signals
- Traps
- Inter-process Communication

Process management

Managing processes is very important because processes are what consumes system resources. System users should be careful about the processes they are creating, in order to ensure that a process is not affecting any other critical processes.

Process creation and execution

In bash, creating a process is very easy. When a program is executed, a new process is created. In a Linux or Unix-based system, when a new process is created, a unique ID is assigned to it, which is known as PID. A PID value is always a positive number starting from 1. Depending upon a system having init or systemd, they always get the PID value 1 because this will be the first process in a system and it is the ancestor of all other processes.

The maximum value of PID is defined in the pid_max file, which should be available in the /proc/sys/kernel/ directory. By default, the pid_max file contains the value 32768 (max PID + 1), which means a maximum of 32767 processes can exist in a system simultaneously. We can change the value of the pid_max file depending upon needs.

For understanding the process creation better, we will create a new process vi from bash:

```
$ vi hello.txt
```

Here, we have created a new process vi that opens the hello.txt file in editor to read and write text. Calling the vi command causes the binary file /usr/bin/vi to execute and perform the needed tasks. A process that creates another process is known as the parent of the process. In this example, vi was created from bash, so bash is the parent of the process vi. The method of creating a child process is known as forking. During the process of fork, a child process inherits the properties of its parents such as GID, real and effective UID and GID, environment variables, shared memory, and resource limit.

To know the PID of the vi process created in the preceding section, we can use the commands such as pidof and ps. For example, run the following command in a new terminal to know the pid of the vi process:

```
$ pidof vi   # Process ID of vi process
21552
$ ps -o ppid= -p 21552      # Knowing parent PID of vi process
1785
```

Once a task is completed, a process gets terminated and PID is free to get assigned to a new process based on need.

The detailed information about each process is available in the `/proc/` directory. A directory with the PID name gets created for each process in `/proc/` containing its detailed information.

A process can be in any of the following states during its lifetime:

- **Running**: In this state, a process is either running or ready to run
- **Waiting**: A process is waiting for a resource
- **Stopped**: A process has been stopped; for example, after receiving a signal
- **Zombie**: A process has exited successfully, but its state change wasn't yet acknowledged by the parent

Process termination

In normal circumstances, after completing tasks, a process terminates and frees up the allocated resources. If the shell has forked any subprocesses, then it will wait for them to finish their task first (other than a background process). In some cases, a process may not behave normally and it can be waiting or consuming resources for a longer time than expected. In some other cases, it may happen that a process is now no longer required. In such cases, we can kill the process from a terminal and free up resources.

To terminate a process, we can use the `kill` command. The `killall` and `pkill` commands can also be used if available on a system.

Using the kill command

The `kill` command sends the specified signal to the specified processes. If no signal is provided, the default `SIGTERM` signal is sent. We will see more about signals further down in this chapter.

The following is the syntax of using the `kill` command:

```
kill PID
```

AND

```
kill -signal PID
```

To kill a process, first get the PID of that process as follows:

```
$ pidof firefox    # Getting PID of firefox process if running
1663
$ kill 1663     # Firefox will be terminated
$ vi hello.txt  # Starting a vi process
$ pidof vi
22715
$ kill -SIGSTOP 22715 # Sending signal to stop vi process
[1]+  Stopped                 vi
```

Here, we used the SIGSTOP signal to stop the process instead of killing it. To kill, we can use the SIGKILL signal or the associated value to this signal, which is 9.

```
$ kill -9 22715  # Killing vi process
```

OR

```
$ kill -SIGKILL 22715  # Killing vi process
```

Using the killall command

It's easy to remember a process by name rather than by PID. The killall command makes it easier to kill a process since it takes the command name as a parameter to kill a process.

The following is the syntax of the killall command:

```
killall process_name
```

AND

```
killall -signal process_name
```

For example, we can kill the firefox process by name, as follows:

```
$ killall firefox  # Firefox application gets terminated
```

Using the pkill command

The pkill command can also be used to kill a process by its name. Unlike the killall command, by default the pkill command finds all the processes beginning with the name specified in its argument.

For example, the following command demonstrates how pkill kills the firefox process from its partial name specified in an argument:

```
$ pkill firef    # Kills processes beginning with name firef and hence
firefox
```

The `pkill` command should be used carefully because it will kill all the matching processes, which may not be our intention. We can determine which processes are going to be killed by `pkill`, using the `pgrep` command with the `-1` option. The `pgrep` command finds processes based on its name and attributes. Run the following commands to list all process names and its PID whose name begin with the `firef` and `fire` strings, respectively:

```
$ pgrep firef
    8168 firefox
```

Here, `firefox` is the matching process name and its PID is `8168`:

```
$ pgrep fire
    747 firewalld
    8168 firefox
```

We can also tell `pkill` to kill a process with exact match of process name using the `--exact` or `-x` option as follows:

```
$ pgrep -x -1  firef  # No match found
$ pkill -x fire  # Nothing gets killed
$ pgrep --exact -1 firefox   # Process firefox found
8168 firefox
$ pkill --exact firefox  # Process firefox will be killed
```

The pkill command can also send a specific signal to all matching processes with the `-signal_name` option as follows:

```
$  pkill -SIGKILL firef
```

The preceding command sends the `SIGKILL` signal to all processes whose name begins with `firef`.

Listing and monitoring processes

In a running system, we often notice that suddenly a system is responding slowly. This can be because a running application is consuming a lot of memory or a process is doing CPU-intensive work. It's hard to predict which application is causing the system to respond slower. To know the reason, it is good to know what all processes are running and also know the monitoring behavior (such as the amount of CPU or memory being consumed) of processes.

Listing processes

To know a list of processes running in the system, we can use the `ps` command.

Syntax

The syntax of the `ps` command is as follows:

```
ps [option]
```

There are a lot of options to use the `ps` command. The commonly used options are explained in the following table.

Simple process selection

The following table shows the multiple options that can be clubbed together and used to get a better selection of results:

Option	Description
-A, -e	Selects all processes
-N	Selects all processes that don't fulfill a condition—that is, negate selection
T	Selects the processes associated with the current terminal
r	Restricts selection to only running processes
x	Selects processes that have no controlling terminal such as daemons launched during booting
a	Selects the processes on a terminal including all users

Process selection by list

The following options accept a single argument in the form of a blank-separated or comma-separated list; they can be used multiple times:

Option	Description
-C cmdlist	Selects the process by its name. The list of names for selection is provided in `cmdlist`.
-g grplist	Selects the process by an effective group name provided in the list of the `grplist` arguments.
-G grplist	Selects the process by a real group name provided in the list of the `grplist` arguments.
-p pidlist	Selects the process by its PID mentioned in `pidlist`.
-t ttylist	Selects the process by a terminal mentioned in `ttylist`.

Option	Description
`-U userlist`	Selects the process by a real user ID or name mentioned in `userlist`.
`-u userlist`	Selects the process by an effective user ID or name mentioned in `userlist`.

Output format control

The following options are used to choose how to display the `ps` command output:

Option	Description
`-j`	Shows the job format.
`-f`	This is used for a full format listing. It also prints the argument passed to the command.
`u`	Displays user-oriented format.
`-l`	Displays long format.
`v`	Displays the virtual memory format.

Listing all processes with details

To know all processes on a system, the `-e` option can be used. To have a more detailed output, use it with the `u` option:

```
$ ps -e u | wc -l     # Total number of processes in system
211
$ ps -e u | tail -n5  # Display only last 5 line of result
```

```
skumari   6940  0.0  0.3 439244 28604 ?      S    13:06   0:00 kdeinit4: kio_http [k e
skumari   6941  0.0  0.3 439244 28604 ?      S    13:06   0:00 kdeinit4: kio_http [k e
root      6976  0.0  0.0      0     0 ?      S    13:09   0:00 [kworker/0:2]
skumari   6981  0.0  0.0 153188  3860 pts/1  R+   13:09   0:00 ps -e u
skumari   6982  0.0  0.0 109544  1880 pts/1  S+   13:09   0:00 tail -n5
```

We can see from the output that all users' processes are displayed. The command that is actually displaying the output—that is, **ps -e u | tail -n5**—is also mentioned in the `ps` output as two separate running processes.

In BSD style, use the `aux` option to get the result that we get from `-e u`:

```
$ ps aux
```

On a Linux-based operating system, aux as well as `-e u` options will work fine.

Listing all processes run by a user

To know which processes are being by a specific user, use the -u option followed by the username. Multiple usernames can also be provided separated by a comma (,).

```
$ ps u -u root | wc -l
130
$ ps u -u root | tail -n5  # Display last 5 results
```

The preceding command displays the following result:

```
root    6506  0.0  0.0    0    0 ?    S  12:29  0:00 [kworker/3:1]
root    6683  0.0  0.0    0    0 ?    S  12:51  0:00 [kworker/0:0]
root    6716  0.0  0.0    0    0 ?    S  12:52  0:00 [kworker/2:0]
root    6795  0.0  0.0    0    0 ?    S  12:59  0:00 [kworker/0:1]
root    6813  0.0  0.0    0    0 ?    S  13:00  0:00 [kworker/u16:1]
```

We see that all processes are running as the user root. The rest of the users' processes have been filtered out.

Processes running in the current terminal

It is useful to know which processes are running in the current terminal. It can help in deciding whether to kill a running terminal or not. We can make a list of processes running in the current terminal using the T or t option.

```
$ ps ut
```

The output for the following command as follows:

```
USER      PID %CPU %MEM    VSZ   RSS TTY   STAT START   TIME COMMAND
skumari  1627  0.0  0.0 118680  5348 pts/1  Ss  Sep04   0:00 /bin/bash
skumari  7329  0.0  0.0 153188  3852 pts/1  R+  13:27   0:00 ps uT
```

We can see from the output that bash and the ps uT command (which we just executed to display the result) are only running processes in the current terminal.

Listing processes by a command name

We can also know process details by its name using the -C option followed by the command name. Multiple command names can be separated by a comma (,):

```
$ ps u -C firefox,bash
```

The following output is obtained:

```
USER       PID %CPU %MEM     VSZ     RSS TTY      STAT START    TIME COMMAND
skumari   1627  0.0  0.0  118680    5348 pts/1    Ss   Sep04    0:00 /bin/bash
skumari   1663  5.6 19.7 3058040 1548424 ?        Sl   Sep04   54:07 /usr/lib64/firefox/firefox
skumari   5668  0.0  0.0  118680    4960 pts/2    Ss+  11:31    0:00 /bin/bash
```

Tree format display of processes

The pstree command displays running processes in a tree structure, which makes it very easy to understand the parent and child relationship of processes.

Running the pstree command with the -p option shows processes in the tree format with its PID number as follows:

```
$ pstree -p
```

```
systemd(1)─┬─NetworkManager(771)─┬─dhclient(8980)
           │                     ├─{NetworkManager}(783)
           │                     ├─{gdbus}(793)
           │                     └─{gmain}(789)
           ├─abrt-dump-journ(1076)
           ├─abrt-watch-log(1079)
           ├─abrtd(711)───{gdbus}(1075)
           ├─accounts-daemon(672)─┬─{gdbus}(684)
           │                      └─{gmain}(682)
           ├─alsactl(659)
           ├─at-spi-bus-laun(1649)─┬─dbus-daemon(1662)───{dbus-daemon}(1666)
           │                       ├─{gdbus}(1657)
           │                       └─{gmain}(1664)
           ├─at-spi2-registr(1671)───{gdbus}(1683)
           ├─atd(798)
           ├─auditd(646)───{auditd}(655)
           ├─avahi-daemon(662)───avahi-daemon(671)
           ├─bluetoothd(691)
           ├─choqok(1591)
           ├─chronyd(665)
           ├─colord(1375)─┬─{gdbus}(1377)
           │              └─{gmain}(1380)
           ├─crond(799)
           ├─cupsd(1865)
```

From the pstree output, we see that the parent process of all processes is systemd. This is started as the first process that is responsible for executing the rest of the processes. In parenthesis, the PID number of each process is mentioned. We can see that the systemd process got PID 1 that is always fixed. On the init based-operating system, init will be the parent of all processes and have PID 1.

To see processes process the tree of a particular PID, we can use `pstree` with the PID number as an argument:

```
$ pstree -p 1627  # Displays process tree of PID 1627 with PID number
```

```
bash(1627)──bash(10706)──┬bash(10734)──less(10759)
                         ├cat(10732)
                         └less(10733)
```

Use the `pstree` command with the `-u` option to see when the UID of the process and parent differs:

```
$ pstree -pu 1627
```

```
bash(1627,skumari)──bash(10706)──┬bash(10734)──┬less(10769)
                                 │             ├sudo(10768,root)
                                 │             └sudo(10787,root)──grep(10788)
                                 ├cat(10732)
                                 └less(10733)
```

We can see that initially, `bash` is being run by the user `skumari` with the PID `1627`. Further down in the tree, the `sudo` command is running as a root.

Monitoring processes

It is very important to know how much memory and CPU a process is consuming while running, in order to ensure there is no leak of memory and over-CPU computation happening. There are commands such as `top`, `htop`, and `vmstat` that can be used to monitor the memory and CPU consumed by each process. Here, we will discuss the `top` command because it is preinstalled in a Linux-based operating system.

The `top` command displays the dynamic real-time usage of the CPU, memory, swap, and the number of tasks currently running with their state.

Running `top` without any options gives the following result:

```
$ top
```

```
top - 23:06:06 up 1 day,  1:27,  2 users,  load average: 0.14, 0.17, 0.20
Tasks: 216 total,   1 running, 210 sleeping,   4 stopped,   1 zombie
%Cpu(s):  4.0 us,  0.9 sy,  0.0 ni, 94.8 id,  0.3 wa,  0.0 hi,  0.0 si,  0.0 st
KiB Mem :  7852744 total,   378972 free,  2802984 used,  4670788 buff/cache
KiB Swap:        0 total,        0 free,        0 used.  4327320 avail Mem

  PID USER      PR  NI    VIRT    RES    SHR S  %CPU %MEM     TIME+ COMMAND
 1663 skumari   20   0 3362056 1.771g 459232 S  13.0 23.7  99:23.84 firefox
  862 root      20   0  866832 489540 450960 S   2.7  6.2  16:52.23 Xorg
 1492 skumari   20   0 3117156  92720  55536 S   2.0  1.2   9:34.01 kwin_x11
 9220 skumari   20   0 5163732 226144  91108 S   1.7  2.9   7:32.73 plasmashell
 2174 skumari   20   0  925032 108304  53196 S   0.7  1.4   7:19.49 plugin-containe
11986 skumari   20   0  453372  42756  36700 S   0.7  0.5   0:00.12 ksnapshot
 1361 skumari   20   0  607888  30248  25792 S   0.3  0.4   0:02.20 klauncher
 1488 skumari   20   0  657624  48496  32388 S   0.3  0.6   0:04.53 ksmserver
 1588 skumari   20   0  593968  51848  42320 S   0.3  0.7   0:58.96 yakuake
 1602 skumari   20   0  609740  49644  37864 S   0.3  0.6   0:12.42 ktorrent
 3270 skumari   20   0 2027736 236988 123960 S   0.3  3.0   1:32.13 soffice.bin
    1 root      20   0  128524   8452   5588 S   0.0  0.1   0:02.87 systemd
    2 root      20   0       0      0      0 S   0.0  0.0   0:00.03 kthreadd
    3 root      20   0       0      0      0 S   0.0  0.0   0:00.15 ksoftirqd/0
    5 root       0 -20       0      0      0 S   0.0  0.0   0:00.00 kworker/0:0H
    7 root      20   0       0      0      0 S   0.0  0.0   0:07.59 rcu_sched
    8 root      20   0       0      0      0 S   0.0  0.0   0:00.00 rcu_bh
    9 root      20   0       0      0      0 S   0.0  0.0   0:05.04 rcuos/0
```

In the `top` command output, the first line tells us about the length of time since the system last booted, the number of users, and the load average.

The second line tells us about the number of tasks and their statuses — running, sleeping, stopped, and zombie.

The third line gives us the details of the CPU usage in percentage. The different CPU usages are shown in the following table:

Value	Description
us	% of the CPU time spent in running un-niced user processes
sy	% of the CPU time spent in kernel space — that is running kernel processes
ni	% of the CPU time running niced user processes
id	% of the time spent idle
wa	% of the time spent waiting for the I/O completion
hi	% of the time spent servicing the hardware interrupt
si	% of the time spent servicing the software interrupts
st	% of the time consumed by a virtual machine

The fourth line tells us about the total, free, used, and buffered RAM memory usage.

The fifth line tells us about the total, free and used swap memory.

The remaining lines give the detailed information about running processes. The meaning of each column is described in the following table:

Column	Description
PID	Process ID
USER	Effective user name of task's owner
PR	Priority of task (lower the value, more is the priority)
NI	Nice value of task. Negative nice value means more priority and positive means lesser priority
VIRT	Virtual memory size used by process
RES	Non-swapped physical memory a process
SHR	Amount of shared memory available to a process
S	Process status – D (uninterruptible sleep), R (Running), S(Sleeping), T (Stopped by job control signal), t (Stopped by debugger), Z (Zombie)
%CPU	% of CPU currently used by process
%MEM	% of Physical memory currently used by process
TIME+	CPU Time, hundredths
COMMAND	Command name

We can also reorder and modify the output when the top is running. To see help, use the *?* or *h* key and the help window will be displayed, which contains following details:

```
Help for Interactive Commands - procps-ng version 3.3.10
Window 1:Def: Cumulative mode Off.   System: Delay 2.0 secs; Secure mode Off.

  Z,B,E,e  Global: 'Z' colors; 'B' bold; 'E'/'e' summary/task memory scale
  l,t,m    Toggle Summary: 'l' load avg; 't' task/cpu stats; 'm' memory info
  0,1,2,3,I Toggle: '0' zeros; '1/2/3' cpus or numa node views; 'I' Irix mode
  f,F,X    Fields: 'f'/'F' add/remove/order/sort; 'X' increase fixed-width

  L,&,<,> . Locate: 'L'/'&' find/again; Move sort column: '<'/'>' left/right
  R,H,V,J . Toggle: 'R' Sort; 'H' Threads; 'V' Forest view; 'J' Num justify
  c,i,S,j . Toggle: 'c' Cmd name/line; 'i' Idle; 'S' Time; 'j' Str justify
  x,y      . Toggle highlights: 'x' sort field; 'y' running tasks
  z,b      . Toggle: 'z' color/mono; 'b' bold/reverse (only if 'x' or 'y')
  u,U,o,O . Filter by: 'u'/'U' effective/any user; 'o'/'O' other criteria
  n,#,^O  . Set: 'n'/'#' max tasks displayed; Show: Ctrl+'O' other filter(s)
  C,...   . Toggle scroll coordinates msg for: up,down,left,right,home,end

  k,r      Manipulate tasks: 'k' kill; 'r' renice
  d or s   Set update interval
  W,Y      Write configuration file 'W'; Inspect other output 'Y'
  q        Quit
           ( commands shown with '.' require a visible task display window )
Press 'h' or '?' for help with Windows,
Type 'q' or <Esc> to continue ▮
```

To sort on the basis of a specific field, the easiest method is to press the *f* key while `top` is running. A new window opens showing all the columns. The opened window looks as follows:

```
Fields Management for window 1:Def, whose current sort field is %CPU
      Navigate with Up/Dn, Right selects for move then <Enter> or Left commits,
      'd' or <Space> toggles display, 's' sets sort.  Use 'q' or <Esc> to end!

* PID      = Process Id            vMj     = Major Faults delta
* USER     = Effective User Name   vMn     = Minor Faults delta
* PR       = Priority              USED    = Res+Swap Size (KiB)
* NI       = Nice Value            nsIPC   = IPC namespace Inode
* VIRT     = Virtual Image (KiB)   nsMNT   = MNT namespace Inode
* RES      = Resident Size (KiB)   nsNET   = NET namespace Inode
* SHR      = Shared Memory (KiB)   nsPID   = PID namespace Inode
* S        = Process Status        nsUSER  = USER namespace Inode
* %CPU     = CPU Usage             nsUTS   = UTS namespace Inode
* %MEM     = Memory Usage (RES)
* TIME+    = CPU Time, hundredths
* COMMAND  = Command Name/Line
  PPID     = Parent Process pid
  UID      = Effective User Id
  RUID     = Real User Id
  RUSER    = Real User Name
```

Use the up and down arrows to navigate and select a column. To sort on the basis of a particular field, press the *s* key and then press *q* to switch back to the top output window.

Here, we have selected NI and then pressed the *s* key and the *q* key. Now, the `top` output will be sorted with `nice` number. The output of the top after sorting with the column **NI** looks as follows:

```
top - 00:45:34 up 1 day,  3:06,  2 users,  load average: 0.07, 0.18, 0.21
Tasks: 219 total,   1 running, 213 sleeping,   4 stopped,   1 zombie
%Cpu(s):  5.2 us,  1.4 sy,  0.0 ni, 93.2 id,  0.3 wa,  0.0 hi,  0.0 si,  0.0 st
KiB Mem :  7852744 total,   871408 free,  3062076 used,  3919260 buff/cache
KiB Swap:        0 total,        0 free,        0 used.  4062792 avail Mem

  PID USER      PR  NI    VIRT    RES    SHR S  %CPU %MEM     TIME+ COMMAND
   40 root      39  19       0      0      0 S   0.0  0.0   0:00.00 khugepaged
  659 root      39  19   16784   2620   2356 S   0.0  0.0   0:00.01 alsactl
   39 root      25   5       0      0      0 S   0.0  0.0   0:00.00 ksmd
  666 rtkit     21   1  164636   2240   2048 S   0.0  0.0   0:00.32 rtkit-daemon
    1 root      20   0  128524   8452   5588 S   0.0  0.1   0:02.96 systemd
    2 root      20   0       0      0      0 S   0.0  0.0   0:00.03 kthreadd
    3 root      20   0       0      0      0 S   0.0  0.0   0:00.16 ksoftirqd/0
    7 root      20   0       0      0      0 S   0.0  0.0   0:08.72 rcu_sched
```

Process substitution

We know that we can use a pipe to provide the output of a command as an input to another command. For example:

```
$ cat file.txt | less
```

Here, the `cat` command output — that is, the content of `file.txt` — is passed to the less command as an input. We can redirect the output of only one process (cat process in this example) as an input to another process.

We may need to feed the output of multiple processes as an input to another process. In such a case, process substitution is used. Process substitution allows a process to take the input from the output of one or more processes rather than a file.

The syntax of using process substitution is as follows:

To substitute input file(s) by list

```
<(list)
```

OR

To substitute output file(s) by list

```
>(list)
```

Here, `list` is a command or a pipeline of commands. Process substitution makes a list act like a file, which is done by giving list a name and then substituting that name in the command line.

Diffing the output of two processes

To compare two sets of data, we use the `diff` command. However, we know that the `diff` command takes two files as an input for producing diff. So, we will have to first save the two sets of data into two separate files and then run `diff`. Saving the content for diff adds extra steps, which is not good. To solve this problem, we can use the process substitution feature while performing `diff`.

For example, we want to know the hidden files in a directory. In a Linux and Unix-based system, files that starts with . (dot) are known as hidden files. To see the hidden files, the `-a` option is used with the `ls` command:

```
$ ls -l ~    # Long list home directory content excluding hidden files
$ ls -al ~   # Long list home directory content including hidden files
```

To get only the hidden files in a directory, run the `diff` command on the sorted output obtained from the preceding two commands:

```
$ diff <(ls -l ~ | tr -s " " | sort -k9) <(ls -al ~ | tr -s " " | sort
-k9)
```

```
1a2,5
> drwxrwxr-x. 8 skumari skumari 220 Sep 7 23:23 .
> drwxrwxrwt. 21 root root 680 Sep 7 23:43 ..
> drwxrwxr-x. 2 skumari skumari 40 Sep 7 23:15 .cache
> drwxrwxr-x. 2 skumari skumari 40 Sep 7 23:15 .cups
4a9,12
> drwxrwxr-x. 2 skumari skumari 40 Sep 7 23:15 .mozilla
> drwxrwxr-x. 2 skumari skumari 40 Sep 7 23:15 .ssh
> -rw-rw-r--. 1 skumari skumari 0 Sep 7 23:16 .viminfo
> -rw-rw-r--. 1 skumari skumari 0 Sep 7 23:16 .xsession-errors
```

Here, we have fed the commands `ls -l ~ | tr -s " " | sort -k9` and `ls -al ~ | tr -s " " | sort -k9` as input data to the `diff` command instead of passing the two files.

Process scheduling priorities

During a process lifetime, it may need CPU and other resources to keep executing normally. We know that multiple processes are running simultaneously in a system and they may need a CPU to complete an operation. To share the available CPUs and resources, process scheduling is done so that each process gets a chance to make use of the CPU. When a process gets created, an initial priority value is set. Depending upon the priority value, the process gets the CPU time.

The process scheduling priority range is from -20 to 19. This value is also called a nice value. The lower the nice value, the higher is the scheduling priority of a process. So, the process with -20 will have the highest scheduling priority and the process with the nice value 19 will have the lowest scheduling priority.

To see the nice value of a process, the `ps` or `top` command can be used. The corresponding nice value of a process is available in the NI column:

```
$ ps -l
```

```
F S   UID   PID  PPID  C PRI  NI ADDR SZ WCHAN  TTY          TIME CMD
0 S  1000  1620  1584  0  80   0 - 29670 wait   pts/1    00:00:00 bash
0 R  1000  3987  1620  0  80   0 - 37772 -      pts/1    00:00:00 ps
```

In the `ps` output, we can see in the NI column that the nice value of bash and the `ps` processes is 0.

Changing scheduling priorities

Every process in a system has some priority assigned that depends upon its nice value. Based on priority, the process gets CPU time and other resources to use. Sometimes, it may happen that a process needs to be executed quickly, but it is waiting for CPU resources to be freed for long time because of a lower scheduling priority. In such cases, we may want to increase its scheduling priority in order to finish a task sooner. We can change the scheduling priority of a process by using the `nice` and `renice` commands.

Using nice

The `nice` command launches a process with a user-defined scheduling priority. By default, processes created by a user get the nice value `0`. To verify this, run the `nice` command without any option:

```
$ nice

0
```

Let's create a new `firefox` process that actually consumes CPU and resources:

```
$ killall firefox  # Terminate any firefox if already running

$ firefox &     # Firefox launched in background

$ top
```

```
top - 22:44:30 up  3:24,  2 users,  load average: 0.13, 0.27, 0.30
Tasks: 216 total,   1 running, 210 sleeping,   4 stopped,   1 zombie
%Cpu(s):  4.9 us,  3.2 sy,  0.0 ni, 91.7 id,  0.3 wa,  0.0 hi,  0.0 si,  0.0 st
KiB Mem :  7852744 total,  4108372 free,  1899432 used,  1844940 buff/cache
KiB Swap:        0 total,        0 free,        0 used.  5475520 avail Mem

  PID USER      PR  NI    VIRT    RES    SHR S  %CPU %MEM     TIME+ COMMAND
 1505 skumari   20   0 4564164 280208  91628 S  12.0  3.6   7:20.05 plasmashell
  863 root      20   0  666532 226088 194692 S   9.0  2.9   7:20.13 Xorg
 1672 skumari   20   0 2189352 815052 157404 S   8.7 10.4  19:30.81 firefox
 1497 skumari   20   0 3113436  89088  54616 S   3.3  1.1   2:35.58 kwin_x11
 1584 skumari   20   0  592844  49596  40636 S   0.7  0.6   0:08.20 yakuake
```

We can see that the nice value of `firefox` is `0` and the CPU usage is 8.7%.

Now, we will kill the current `firefox` and launch another `firefox` with the nice value `10`. This means, `firefox` will have a lower priority than other user-created processes.

To create a process with a different nice value, the `-n` option is used with `nice`:

```
$ killall firefox
$ nice -n 10 firefox &
```

OR

```
$ nice -10 firefox &
```

To see what nice value `firefox` has now, check the `top` output:

```
$ top
```

```
top - 22:57:59 up  3:37,  3 users,  load average: 0.12, 0.36, 0.33
Tasks: 217 total,   1 running, 209 sleeping,   6 stopped,   1 zombie
%Cpu(s):  3.7 us,  3.1 sy,  0.8 ni, 92.2 id,  0.3 wa,  0.0 hi,  0.0 si,  0.0 st
KiB Mem :  7852744 total,  4539276 free,  1446520 used,  1866948 buff/cache
KiB Swap:        0 total,        0 free,        0 used.  6042240 avail Mem

  PID USER      PR  NI    VIRT    RES    SHR S  %CPU %MEM     TIME+ COMMAND
 1505 skumari   20   0 5203304 295492  99932 S  14.3  3.8   8:17.04 plasmashell
  863 root      20   0  461944 146024 114252 S   8.6  1.9   7:57.08 Xorg
 5860 skumari   30  10 1246200 352664 104852 S   4.7  4.5   0:05.07 firefox
 1497 skumari   20   0 3113320  89048  54324 S   3.0  1.1   2:47.04 kwin_x11
 5953 skumari   20   0  454076  43156  36532 S   1.3  0.5   0:00.17 ksnapshot
```

We can see that the `firefox` process has the `10` nice value. To provide more scheduling priority — that is, setting a negative nice value to a process — root privilege is required.

The following example sets the `firefox` process as a higher scheduling priority:

```
$  nice -n -10 firefox
```

OR

```
$ sudo  nice --10 firefox
```

Using renice

The `nice` command can only modify a nice value during the launch of a process. However, if we want to change a running process scheduling priority, then the `renice` command should be used. The `renice` command alters the scheduling priority of one or more running processes.

The syntax of using `renice` is as follows:

```
renice [-n] priority [-g|-p|-u] identifier
```

Here, the -g option considers succeeding an argument—that is, identifier as GIDs.

The -p option considers succeeding an argument—that is, identifier as PIDs.

The -u option considers succeeding an argument—that is, identifier as usernames or UIDs.

If none of the options— -g, -p, or -u—are provided, identifiers are considered as PIDs.

For example, we will change the priority of all the processes belonging to a user. Firstly, see the current priority of processes owned by the user:

```
$ top -u skumari     # User is skumari
```

PID	USER	PR	NI	VIRT	RES	SHR	S	%CPU	%MEM	TIME+	COMMAND
1505	skumari	20	0	5205352	297680	101604	S	45.0	3.8	10:58.82	plasmashell
5969	skumari	20	0	1357460	459964	108340	S	5.0	5.9	1:35.55	firefox
1497	skumari	20	0	3115036	90048	54828	S	4.7	1.1	3:10.34	kwin_x11
6409	skumari	20	0	453804	43096	36788	S	2.3	0.5	0:00.23	ksnapshot
1584	skumari	20	0	593648	50616	40696	S	0.7	0.6	0:13.98	yakuake
2064	skumari	20	0	2210268	229864	114260	S	0.7	2.9	0:40.01	soffice.bin
1483	skumari	20	0	598832	31780	27368	S	0.3	0.4	0:00.62	kaccess
1588	skumari	20	0	660228	139944	69468	S	0.3	1.8	0:14.53	choqok
1635	skumari	20	0	1293448	51596	39660	S	0.3	0.7	0:00.84	knotify4
1262	skumari	20	0	44996	4740	4124	S	0.0	0.1	0:00.03	systemd
1264	skumari	20	0	84128	2936	0	S	0.0	0.0	0:00.00	(sd-pam)
1266	skumari	20	0	0	0	0	Z	0.0	0.0	0:00.01	kwalletd
1267	skumari	20	0	114856	3064	2800	S	0.0	0.0	0:00.01	startkde
1282	skumari	20	0	16064	1564	1360	S	0.0	0.0	0:00.00	dbus-launch
1283	skumari	20	0	63364	4196	2672	S	0.0	0.1	0:01.03	dbus-daemon
1297	skumari	20	0	53408	572	0	S	0.0	0.0	0:00.02	ssh-agent
1350	skumari	20	0	414836	26336	22200	S	0.0	0.3	0:00.23	kwalletd
1353	skumari	20	0	11972	2764	2576	S	0.0	0.0	0:00.00	gam_server

Now, we will modify the priority of all processes using renice with the -u option:

```
$ sudo renice -n -5 -u skumari
```

Let's view a new nice value of processes owned by the user `skumari`:

```
$ top -u skumari
```

PID	USER	PR	NI	VIRT	RES	SHR	S	%CPU	%MEM	TIME+	COMMAND
1505	skumari	15	-5	5205272	297616	101492	S	7.6	3.8	12:04.73	plasmashell
5969	skumari	15	-5	1357588	459712	108340	S	6.3	5.9	2:04.20	firefox
6555	skumari	15	-5	453352	42408	36368	S	4.0	0.5	0:00.12	ksnapshot
1497	skumari	15	-5	3114868	90012	54668	S	2.7	1.1	3:20.00	kwin_x11
1361	skumari	15	-5	2045860	94012	66452	S	0.7	1.2	0:05.25	kded5
1584	skumari	15	-5	593648	50632	40696	S	0.7	0.6	0:15.24	yakuake
1359	skumari	15	-5	607876	30756	26276	S	0.3	0.4	0:00.62	klauncher
1399	skumari	15	-5	815544	34748	30444	S	0.3	0.4	0:00.83	kactivitymanage
1483	skumari	15	-5	598832	31780	27368	S	0.3	0.4	0:00.66	kaccess
1488	skumari	15	-5	657484	48212	32208	S	0.3	0.6	0:01.20	ksmserver
1843	skumari	15	-5	585212	34964	30888	S	0.3	0.4	0:00.99	kwalletd5
2064	skumari	15	-5	2212472	232092	114260	S	0.3	3.0	0:44.59	soffice.bin
6066	skumari	15	-5	559348	54044	42336	S	0.3	0.7	0:02.68	plugin-containe
1262	skumari	15	-5	44996	4740	4124	S	0.0	0.1	0:00.03	systemd
1264	skumari	15	-5	84128	2936	0	S	0.0	0.0	0:00.00	(sd-pam)
1266	skumari	15	-5	0	0	0	Z	0.0	0.0	0:00.01	kwalletd
1267	skumari	15	-5	114856	3064	2800	S	0.0	0.0	0:00.01	startkde

To modify the scheduling priority of a few processes, modify using the process's PIDs. The following example modifies the process plasmashell and Firefox having the PIDs `1505` and `5969` respectively:

```
$ sudo renice -n 2 -p 1505 5969
```

```
$ top -u skumari
```

PID	USER	PR	NI	VIRT	RES	SHR	S	%CPU	%MEM	TIME+	COMMAND
1505	skumari	22	2	5205440	297740	101648	S	43.3	3.8	12:41.93	plasmashell
5969	skumari	22	2	1357716	460692	108340	S	4.3	5.9	2:26.84	firefox
1497	skumari	15	-5	3114900	90052	54708	S	4.0	1.1	3:26.72	kwin_x11
1584	skumari	15	-5	593648	50636	40696	S	0.7	0.6	0:16.07	yakuake

Now, we can see that the nice values of the process plasmashell and Firefox are 2.

Signals

A signal is a software interrupt to notify processes that an external event has occurred. In a normal execution, processes keeps running as expected. Now, for some reason, a user may want to cancel a running `process`. When the process is started from a terminal, it will terminate when we hit the *Ctrl* + *c* keys or run the `kill` command.

When we press *Ctrl* + *c* keys while process is running in a terminal, a signal `SIGINT` is generated and sent to the process running in foreground. Also, when the `kill` command is called on process, the `SIGKILL` signal is generated and the process is terminated.

Available signals

Among all available signals, we will discuss the frequently used signals here:

Signal name	Value	Default Action	Description
SIGHUP	1	Term	This signal is used to Hangup or death of controlling process
SIGINT	2	Term	This signal is used to interrupt from keyboard like ctrl + c, ctrl + z
SIGQUIT	3	Core	This signal is used to quit from keyboard
SIGILL	4	Core	It is used to for Illegal instruction
SIGTRAP	5	Core	This signal is used to trace or breakpoint trap
SIGABRT	6	Core	It is used to abort signal
SIGFPE	8	Core	Floating point exception
SIGKILL	9	Term	Process terminates immediately
SIGSEGV	11	Core	Invalid memory reference
SIGPIPE	13	Term	Broken pipe
SIGALRM	14	Term	Alarm signal
SIGTERM	15	Term	Terminate the process
SIGCHLD	17	Ign	Child stopped or terminated
SIGSTOP	19	Stop	This signal is used to stop the process
SIGPWR	30	Term	Power failure

In the preceding table, we mentioned the signal name and value. Any of them can be used while referring to a signal. The meaning of terms used in the **Default action** section are as follows:

- Term: Terminate
- Core: Terminate the process and dump core
- Ign: Ignore the signal
- Stop: Stop the process

Depending upon what kind of signal it is, any of the following actions can be taken:

- A signal can be ignored by a process, which means no action will be taken. Most of the signals can be ignored, except SIGKILL and SIGSTOP. The SIGKILL and SIGSTOP signals can't be caught, blocked, or ignored. This allows the kernel to kill or stop any process at any point of time.

- A signal can be handled by writing a signal handler code specifying the required action to be taken after a particular signal is received.

- Each signal has a default action, so let the signal perform the default action; for example, terminate the process in case the SIGKILL signal is sent.

To know all signals and its corresponding value, use the kill command with the -1 option:

```
$ kill -1
```

```
 1) SIGHUP       2) SIGINT       3) SIGQUIT      4) SIGILL       5) SIGTRAP
 6) SIGABRT      7) SIGBUS       8) SIGFPE       9) SIGKILL     10) STGUSR1
11) SIGSEGV     12) SIGUSR2     13) SIGPIPE     14) SIGALRM     15) SIGTERM
16) SIGSTKFLT   17) SIGCHLD     18) SIGCONT     19) SIGSTOP     20) SIGTSTP
21) SIGTTIN     22) SIGTTOU     23) SIGURG      24) SIGXCPU     25) SIGXFSZ
26) SIGVTALRM   27) SIGPROF     28) SIGWINCH    29) SIGIO       30) SIGPWR
31) SIGSYS      34) SIGRTMIN    35) SIGRTMIN+1  36) SIGRTMIN+2  37) SIGRTMIN+3
38) SIGRTMIN+4  39) SIGRTMIN+5  40) SIGRTMIN+6  41) SIGRTMIN+7  42) SIGRTMIN+8
43) SIGRTMIN+9  44) SIGRTMIN+10 45) SIGRTMIN+11 46) SIGRTMIN+12 47) SIGRTMIN+13
48) SIGRTMIN+14 49) SIGRTMIN+15 50) SIGRTMAX-14 51) SIGRTMAX-13 52) SIGRTMAX-12
53) SIGRTMAX-11 54) SIGRTMAX-10 55) SIGRTMAX-9  56) SIGRTMAX-8  57) SIGRTMAX-7
58) SIGRTMAX-6  59) SIGRTMAX-5  60) SIGRTMAX-4  61) SIGRTMAX-3  62) SIGRTMAX-2
63) SIGRTMAX-1  64) SIGRTMAX
```

The kill command also provides a way to convert a signal number to a name when used in the following way:

```
kill -1 signal_number
```

```
$ kill -1 9
KILL
$ kill -1 29
IO
$ kill -1 100  # invalid signal number gives error
bash: kill: 100: invalid signal specification
```

To send a signal to process(es), we can use the kill, pkill, and kilall commands:

```
$ kill -9 6758  # Sends SIGKILL process to PID 6758
$ killall -1 foo  # Sends SIGHUP signal to process foo
$ pkill -19 firef  # Sends SIGSTOP signal to processes' name beginning
with firef
```

Traps

When a process is running and in between we kill the process, the process terminates instantly without doing anything further. A programmer who writes a program may want to do some tasks before a program actually terminates; for example, a clean up of the temporary directories created, saving applications' state, saving logs, and so on. In such a case, a programmer would like to listen to signals and do the required task before actually allowing you to terminate the process.

Consider the following shell script example:

```
#!/bin/bash
# Filename: my_app.sh
# Description: Reverse a file

echo "Enter file to be reversed"
read filename

tmpfile="/tmp/tmpfile.txt"
# tac command is used to print a file in reverse order
tac $filename > $tmpfile
cp $tmpfile $filename
rm $tmpfile
```

This program takes an input from a user file and then reverses the file content. This script creates a temporary file to keep the reversed content of the file and later copies it to the original file. At the end, it deletes the temporary file.

When we execute this script, it may be waiting for a user to input a text filename or maybe in between reversing the file (a large file takes more time to reverse the content). During this, if processes are terminated, then the temporary file may not get deleted. It is the programmer's task to make sure that temporary files are deleted.

To solve such a problem, we can handle the signal, perform the necessary tasks, and then terminate the process. This can be achieved by using the `trap` command. This command allows you to execute a command when a signal is received by a script.

The syntax of using `trap` is as follows:

`$ trap action signals`

Here, we can provide `trap action` to be performed. An action can be an executing command (s).

In the preceding syntax of `trap`, signals refers to providing one or more signal names for which an action has to be performed.

The following shell script demonstrates how trap is used to perform tasks before a process suddenly exits on receiving a signal:

```
#!/bin/bash
# Filename: my_app_with_trap.sh
# Description: Reverse a file and perform action on receiving signals

echo "Enter file to be reversed"
read filename

tmpfile="/tmp/tmpfile.txt"
# Delete temporary file on receiving any of signals
# SIGHUP SIGINT SIGABRT SIGTERM SIGQUIT and then exit from script
trap "rm $tmpfile; exit" SIGHUP SIGINT SIGABRT SIGTERM SIGQUIT
# tac command is used to print a file in reverse order
tac $filename > $tmpfile
cp $tmpfile $filename
rm $tmpfile
```

In this modified script, when any of the signals such as SIGHUP, SIGINT, SIGABRT, SIGTERM, or SIGQUIT are received, then rm $tmpfile; exit will be executed. This means that a temporary file will first be deleted and then you can exit from the script.

Inter-process communication

A process alone can do a certain things, but not everything. It will be a very useful and good resource utilization if two or more processes can communicate with each other in the form of sharing results, sending or receiving messages, and so on. In a Linux or Unix-based operating system, two or more processes can communicate with each other using IPC.

IPC is the technique by which processes communicate with each other and are managed by kernel.

IPC is possible to do by any of the following ways:

- **Named pipes**: These allow processes to read from and write into it.
- **Shared memory**: This is created by one process and is further available for read from and write to this memory by multiple processes.
- **Message queue**: This is a structured and an ordered list of memory segments where processes store or retrieve data in queue fashion.

- **Semaphores**: This provides a synchronizing mechanism for processes that are accessing the same resource. It has counters that are used to control the access to shared resources by multiple processes.

While discussing named pipes in *Chapter 6, Working with Files,* we learned how processes can communicate using named pipes.

Information on IPC using ipcs

The `ipcs` command provides information about IPC facilities for which a calling process has the read access. It can provide information on three resources: shared memory, message queue, and semaphore.

The syntax of using `ipcs` is as follows:

```
ipcs option
```

Where options are as follows:

Option	Description
-a	Displays information for all resources — shared memory, message queue, and semaphore
-q	Displays information about active message queues
-m	Displays information about active shared memory segments
-s	Displays information about active semaphore sets
-i ID	Shows the detailed information for an ID. Use it with the -q, -m or -s option.
-l	Shows resource limits
-p	Shows PIDs of the resource creator and last operator
-b	Prints sizes in bytes
--human	Print sizes in a human-readable format

Listing information provided by IPCs

We can use the `ipcs` command without an option or with –a:

```
$ ipcs
```

OR

```
$ ipcs -a
```

```
------ Message Queues --------
key        msqid      owner      perms      used-bytes    messages

------ Shared Memory Segments --------
key        shmid      owner      perms      bytes         nattch    status
0x6c6c6536 0          root       600        4096          0
0x00000000 393217     skumari    600        4194304       2         dest
0x00000000 622594     skumari    600        900           2         dest
0x00000000 98307      skumari    700        7979520       2         dest
0x00000000 131076     skumari    700        7979520       2         dest
0x00000000 720901     skumari    600        393216        2         dest
0x00000000 1081350    skumari    600        1146320       2         dest
0x00000000 458759     skumari    700        1184260       2         dest
0x00000000 851976     skumari    600        900           2         dest
0x00000000 524297     skumari    600        16777216      2         dest
0x00000000 1245194    skumari    700        6386688       2         dest
0x00000000 917515     skumari    600        134217728     2         dest
0x00000000 1867788    skumari    600        9216          2         dest
0x00000000 1048589    skumari    600        2097152       2         dest
0x00000000 1277966    skumari    700        444928        2         dest
0x00000000 1540111    skumari    600        393216        2         dest

------ Semaphore Arrays --------
key        semid      owner      perms      nsems
```

To see only the shared memory segment, we can use `ipcs` with the `-m` option:

```
$ ipcs -m --human
```

```
------ Shared Memory Segments --------
key        shmid      owner      perms      size       nattch    status
0x6c6c6536 0          root       600        4K         0
0x00000000 393217     skumari    600        4M         2         dest
0x00000000 622594     skumari    600        900B       2         dest
0x00000000 98307      skumari    700        7.6M       2         dest
0x00000000 131076     skumari    700        7.6M       2         dest
0x00000000 720901     skumari    600        384K       2         dest
0x00000000 1081350    skumari    600        1.1M       2         dest
0x00000000 458759     skumari    700        1.1M       2         dest
0x00000000 851976     skumari    600        900B       2         dest
0x00000000 524297     skumari    600        16M        2         dest
0x00000000 1245194    skumari    700        6.1M       2         dest
0x00000000 917515     skumari    600        128M       2         dest
0x00000000 1867788    skumari    600        9K         2         dest
0x00000000 1048589    skumari    600        2M         2         dest
0x00000000 1277966    skumari    700        434.5K     2         dest
0x00000000 1540111    skumari    600        384K       2         dest
```

Here, the `--human` option made a size column in a more readable format by providing the size in KB and MB instead of giving it in bytes.

To find out detailed information about a resource ID, use `ipcs` with the `-i` option followed by the resource ID:

```
$ ipcs -m -i 393217
```

```
Shared memory Segment shmid=393217
uid=1000         gid=1000          cuid=1000         cgid=1000
mode=01600       access_perms=0600
bytes=4194304    lpid=5134         cpid=1774         nattch=2
att_time=Wed Sep   9 23:37:14 2015
det_time=Wed Sep   9 23:37:14 2015
change_time=Wed Sep   9 19:45:06 2015
```

Knowing processes' PID who recently did IPCs

We can know the PID of the processes that have recently accessed a specific IPC resource using the `-p` option:

```
$ ipcs -m -p
```

```
------ Shared Memory Creator/Last-op PIDs --------
shmid        owner        cpid        lpid
0            root         247         247
393217       skumari      1774        5134
622594       skumari      2074        5134
98307        skumari      1650        5134
131076       skumari      1654        6187
720901       skumari      2125        5134
1081350      skumari      2365        5134
458759       skumari      1631        5134
851976       skumari      2074        5134
524297       skumari      1774        5134
1245194      skumari      1629        5640
917515       skumari      1774        5134
1867788      skumari      4829        858
1048589      skumari      2125        5134
1277966      skumari      1629        5640
1540111      skumari      2125        5134
```

Here, the `cpid` column shows `pid` of the processes that created the shared memory resource, and `lpid` refers to the PID of the processes that last accessed the shared memory resource.

Summary

After reading this chapter, you will understand what process is in a Linux and UNIX-based system. You should now know how to create, stop, terminate, and monitor processes. You should also know how to send signals to a process and manage the received signals in your shell script with the `trap` command. You have also learned how different processes communicate with each other using IPC on mechanism in order to share resources or to send and receive messages.

In the next chapter, you will learn about the different ways in which tasks can be automated and how they run at a specified time without any further human intervention. You will also learn how and why start-up files are created, and how to embed other programming languages such as Python in a shell script.

8

Scheduling Tasks and Embedding Languages in Scripts

Until now, we learned about various useful shell utilities and how to write them into a shell script in order to avoid writing the same instructions again and again. Automating tasks by writing into scripts reduces the tasks up to a certain extent, but still we will have to run those scripts whenever required. Sometimes, it happens that we want to run a command or script at a particular time, for example, sysadmin has to run a clean-up and maintenance of a system available in the data center at 12:30 AM. To perform the required operation, sysadmin will login into a machine around 12:30 AM and do the necessary work. But what if his or her home network is down and the data center is far? It will be inconvenient and tough to perform a task at that moment. There are also a few tasks that need to be performed on daily or hourly basis, for example, monitoring the network usage of each user, taking a system backup, and so on. It will be very boring to execute repetitive tasks again and again.

In this chapter, we will see how to solve such issues by scheduling tasks at a specific time or interval of time by using utilities `at` and `crontab`. We will also see how systemd (the first process started after a system is booted up with PID 1) manages processes needed after system start-up. We will also see how systemd manages different services and system logs. At the end, we will learn how we can embed other scripting languages in a shell script to get extra capabilities in the shell script.

This chapter will cover the following topics in detail:

- Running tasks at a specific time
- Cron jobs
- Managing Crontab entry
- systemd
- Embedding languages

Running tasks at a specific time

In general, when we run a command or script, it starts executing instantly. However, what if we want it to run later at a specific time? For example, I want to download large data from the Internet, but don't want to slow down my Internet bandwidth while I am working. So, I would like to run my download script at 1:00 AM since I won't be using the Internet for any kind of work after 1:00 AM. It is possible to schedule download scripts or commands later at a specified time using the `at` command. We can also list scheduled tasks using the `atq` command or remove any scheduled tasks using the `atrm` command.

Executing scripts using at

We will use the `at` command to run tasks at a given time. The syntax of using the `at` command is as follows:

```
at [Option] specified_time
```

In the preceding syntax, `specified_time` refers to the time at which a command or script should run. The time can be in the following format:

Time format	Description
HH:MM	The specific time of the day in hours (HH) and minutes (MM). If the time is already past, then the next day is assumed. Time is specified in 24 hours format.
noon	At 12:00 during day time.
teatime	At 16:00 or 4 pm in afternoon.
midnight	At 12:00 at night.
today	Refers to the current time on same day.
tomorrow	Refers to the current time on the next day.
AM or PM	Suffixed with the time to specify time in 12-hour format, for example, 4:00PM.

Time format	Description
now + count time-units	Run a script at the same time after a certain time-unit. Count can be an integer number. Time units can be in minutes, hours, days, weeks, months, or years.
Date	A date can be given in the form of month-name, day, and optional year. Date can be in one of the following formats: MMDD[CC]YY, MM/DD/[CC]YY, DD.MM.[CC]YY, or [CC] YY-MM-DD.

The options to the `at` command are explained in the following table:

Option	Description
`-f FILE`	Specify a script file to be executed.
`-l`	Alias to the `atq` command.
`-m`	Send an e-mail to the user on job completion.
`-M`	Don't send an e-mail to the user.
`-r`	Alias to the `atrm` command.
`-t time`	Run a job at the time. The format of time is given as [[CC] YY]MMDDhhmm[.ss].
`-c job_number`	Print the job associated with `job_number` on a standard output.
`-v`	Print the time at which the job will be executed.

Scheduling commands

The following command is scheduled to run at 14:00, which stores the filesystem's usage in a file called `file_system_usage.log` in a user's home directory:

```
$ at 14:00
warning: commands will be executed using /bin/sh
at> df > ~/file_system_usage.log
at> <EOT>
job 33 at Mon Sep 21 14:00:00 2015
```

When we run the `at` command as shown, a warning message **warning: commands will be executed using /bin/sh** is printed, which specifies which shell will be used to execute commands. In the next line, we will see `at` prompt where we can specify the list of commands to be executed at 14:00. In our case, we entered the `df > ~/file_system_usage.log` command, which means run the `df` command and save its result in the `file_system_usage.log` file.

Once the list of commands to be entered is finished, press the *Enter* key and then, in the next line, use the *Ctrl + d* keys to exit from `at` prompt. Before getting a normal shell prompt, we will see the message saying created job number and time stamp at which the job will be executed. In our case, the job number is 33 and the time stamp is `Mon Sep 21 14:00:00 2015`.

We can check the content of the `file_system_usage.log` file once the time stamp we specified is over.

We can print on `stdout` what is going to be executed when a particular scheduled job runs:

```
$ at -c 33   # Lists content of job 33
```

```
PAM_KWALLET_LOGIN=/tmp//skumari.socket; export PAM_KWALLET_LOGIN
XAUTHORITY=/tmp/xauth-1000-_0; export XAUTHORITY
CCACHE_HASHDIR=; export CCACHE_HASHDIR
cd /home/skumari || {
        echo 'Execution directory inaccessible' >&2
        exit 1
}
${SHELL:-/bin/sh} << 'marcinDELIMITER0aeddab2'
df > ~/file_system_usage.log
marcinDELIMITER0aeddab2
```

We can see that the `df > ~/file_system_usage.log` command will be executed. The rest of the lines specify in what environment a task will be executed.

Now, consider a job scheduled by the root user:

```
# at -v 4am
Mon Sep 21 04:00:00 2015


warning: commands will be executed using /bin/sh
at> reboot
at> <EOT>
job 34 at Mon Sep 21 04:00:00 2015
```

The job with the number 34 is scheduled by the user root. This job system will reboot at 4am.

Scheduling a script file

We can schedule a script file for execution at a specific time using the -f option with the at command.

For example, we want to run the loggedin_user_detail.sh script next week at 4 pm. This script lists logged in users and what processes they are running when the script gets executed at a scheduled time. The content of the script is as follows:

```
$ cat  loggedin_user_detail.sh
#!/bin/bash
# Filename: loggedin_user_detail.sh
# Description: Collecting information of loggedin users

users_log_file=~/users_log_file.log
echo "List of logged in users list at time 'date'" > $users_log_file
users=('who | cut -d' ' -f1 | sort | uniq')
echo ${users[*]} >> $users_log_file

for i in ${users[*]}
do
   echo "Processes owned by user $i" >> $users_log_file
   ps u -u $i >> $users_log_file
   echo
done
$ chmod +x  loggedin_user_detail.sh  # Provide execute permission
```

Now, to run the preceding script at 4 pm next week, we will run the following command:

```
$at -f loggedin_user_detail.sh 4pm + 1 week
warning: commands will be executed using /bin/sh
job 42 at Sun Sep 27 16:00:00 2015
```

We can see that the job has been scheduled to run one week later.

Listing scheduled tasks

Sometimes, it happens that a task has been scheduled to run at a specific time, but we forget the time at which a task is supposed to run. We can see the already scheduled tasks using one of the `atq` or the `at` command with the `-l` option:

```
$ atq
33         Mon Sep 21 14:00:00 2015 a skumari
42         Sun Sep 27 16:00:00 2015 a skumari
```

The `atq` command displays jobs scheduled by the current user with the job number, time, and user's name:

```
$ sudo atq
34         Mon Sep 21 04:00:00 2015 a root
33         Mon Sep 21 14:00:00 2015 a skumari
42         Sun Sep 27 16:00:00 2015 a skumari
```

Running `atq` with `sudo`, lists jobs scheduled by all users.

Removing scheduled tasks

We can also remove a scheduled task if the task is no longer required to be performed. Removing a task is also useful when we want to the modify time at which a task is to be executed. To modify time, first remove the scheduled task and then create the same task again with the new time.

For example, we don't want to reboot a system at 1 am instead of 4 am. For this, the root user will first remove the job 34 using the `atrm` command:

```
# atrm 34
$ sudo atq      # Updated lists of tasks
    33         Mon Sep 21 14:00:00 2015 a skumari
    42         Sun Sep 27 16:00:00 2015 a skumari
# at 1am
warning: commands will be executed using /bin/sh
    at> reboot
    at> <EOT>
job 47 at Mon Sep 21 01:00:00 2015
$ sudo atq
```

```
33         Mon Sep 21 14:00:00 2015 a skumari
42         Sun Sep 27 16:00:00 2015 a skumari
47         Mon Sep 21 01:00:00 2015 a root
```

We can see that the task scheduled by the root user will now run at 1 am instead of 4 am.

Cron jobs

Cron jobs are jobs or tasks that run at regular intervals of time unlike the at command. For example, in office, my job is to keep all the detailed information of company employees that is confidential. To keep it secure and updated without any loss of information, I will have to take the backup of the latest data in external devices such as a hard disk or a flash drive. Depending upon the number of employees, I may have to take the backup on a minute, hour, daily or weekly basis. It's hard, tedious, and a waste of time to back up manually every time. By having the knowledge of how to schedule a cron job, it can be very easily achieved. A Cron job creation is frequently done by system administrators to schedule tasks that are to be performed at regular intervals, for example, taking the backup of a system, saving logs of each user who is logged in, monitoring and reporting the network usage of each user, performing system clean-up, scheduling system update, and so on.

Cron consists of two parts: cron daemon and cron configuration.

Cron daemon

The cron daemon automatically starts when a system is booted and keeps running in the background. Daemon process is known as crond and is started by systemd or the init process, depending upon what your system has. Its task is to check configuration files regularly at one minute intervals and check whether any tasks are to be completed.

Cron configuration

Cron configuration contains files and directories where the Cron jobs to be scheduled are written. They are available in the /etc/ directory. The most important file associated with cron configuration is crontab. In a Linux system, configuration files related to cron are as follows:

- /etc/cron.hourly/: This contains the scripts to be run each hour
- /etc/cron.daily/: This contains the scripts to be run once in a day

- `/etc/cron.weekly/`: This contains the scripts to be run once in a week
- `/etc/cron.monthly/`: This contains the scripts to be run once in a month
- `/etc/crontab`: This contains commands and the interval at which they should run
- `/etc/cron.d/`: This is the directory with files having commands and the interval at which they should run

Scripts can be directly added into any of the directories such as `cron.hourly/`, `cron.daily/`, `cron.weekly/`, or `cron.monthly/`, in order to run them at an hourly, daily, weekly, or monthly basis respectively.

The following is a simple shell script `firefox_memcheck.sh`, which checks whether a Firefox process is running or not. If Firefox is running and its memory usage is greater than 30 percent, then restart Firefox:

```
#!/bin/sh
# Filename: firefox_memcheck.sh
# Desription: Resatrts application firefix if memory usage is more
than 30%

pid='pidof firefox' # Get pid of firefox
if [ $pid -gt 1 ]
then
  # Get current memory usage of firefox
  current_mem_usage='ps -u --pid $pid| tail -n1 | tr -s ' ' | cut -d '
' -f 4'
  # Check if firefox memory  usage is more than 30% or not
  if [ $(echo "$current_mem_usage > 30" | bc) -eq 1 ]
  then
     kill $pid   # Kill firefox if memory usage is > 30%
     firefox &   # Launch firefox
  fi
fi
```

We can add this script into the `/etc/cron.hourly/` directory of the system and it will keep checking our Firefox memory usage. This script can be modified to monitor the memory usage for other processes too.

Crontab entries

By putting scripts into cron.{hourly, daily, weekly, monthly}, we can only set tasks at an interval of an hour, day, week, and month. What if a task has to run at 2-day intervals, 10-day intervals, 90 minute intervals, and so on? To achieve this, we can add tasks into the /etc/crontab file or the /etc/cron.d/ directory. Each user may have their own crontab entry and files related to each users are available in /var/spool/.

A crontab entry looks as follows:

```
.---------------- minute (0 - 59)
|  .------------- hour (0 - 23)
|  |  .---------- day of month (1 - 31)
|  |  |  .------- month (1 - 12) OR jan,feb,mar,apr ...
|  |  |  |  .---- day of week (0 - 6) (Sunday=0 or 7) OR sun,mon,tue,wed,thu,fri,sat
|  |  |  |  |
*  *  *  *  * user-name  command to be executed
```

We can see from the preceding screenshot that a crontab entry has five asterisks. Each asterisk defines a specific duration. We can replace * with a value suggested against each of them or leave it as it is. If * is mentioned in a field, then it means consider all the instances of that field.

The timing syntax can also be described as follows:

- Specify the **minutes** value between 0 to 59
- Specify **hours** that can range from 0 to 23
- Specify **days** that can range from 1 to 31
- Specify **months** that can range from 1 to 12 or we can write Jan, Feb, ... Dec
- Specify the **day of a week** that can range from 0 to 6 or we can write sun (0), mon (1), ..., sat (6)

All five fields are separated by blank spaces. It is followed by a **username** that specifies by which user the command will be executed. Specifying the username is optional and by default it is run as a root. The last field is command that is scheduled for execution.

An example demonstrating how to write the crontab entry is as follows:

```
20 7 * * 0 foo command
```

Each field can be explained as follows:

- `20`: 20th minute
- `7`: 7AM
- `*`: Each day
- `*`: Each month
- `0`: On Sunday
- `foo`: This command will run as the foo user
- `command`: This is the specified command to be executed

So, the command will run as root at 7:20 AM every Sunday.

We can specify multiple instances of a filed using a comma (,):

```
30 20,22 * * * command
```

Here, `command` will run at 8:30 PM and 10:30 PM every day.

We can also specify a range of time in a field using a hyphen (-) as follows:

```
35 7-11 * * 0-3 command
```

This means, the run command is at 7:35, 8:35, 9:35, 10:35, and 11:35 on Sunday, Monday, Tuesday, and Wednesday.

To run a script at a specific interval, we can specify the forward slash (/) as follows:

```
20-45/4 8 9 4 * command
```

The command will run on 9th April between 8:20 AM to 8:45 AM at an interval of 4 minutes.

Special strings in Crontab

Crontab may have the following strings specified as well:

String	Description
`@hourly`	Run once in an hour, equivalent to 0 * * * *
`@daily` or `@midnight`	Run once in a day, equivalent to 0 0 * * *
`@weekly`	Run once in a week, equivalent to 0 0 * * 0
`@monthly`	Run once in a month, equivalent to 0 0 1 * *
`@yearly` or `@annually`	Run once in a year, equivalent to 0 0 1 1 *
`@reboot`	Run at system start-up

Managing the crontab entry

We don't add or modify an entry of a crontab directly. It is done by using the crontab command that allows you to add, modify, and list crontab entries. Each user can have their own crontab where they can add, delete, or modify tasks. By default, it is enabled for all users, but if a system administrator wants to restrict some of the users, he or she can add that user in the /etc/cron.deny file.

The syntax of using the crontab command is as follows:

```
crontab [-u user] file
crontab [-u user] [option]
```

The options of the crontab are explained in the following table:

Option	Description
-u user	Appends the name of the user whose crontab is to be modified
-l	Displays the current crontab on stdout
-e	Edit the current crontab using an editor specified by the EDITOR env
-r	Remove the current crontab
-i	Interactive removal of the current crontab when used with the -r option

Listing crontab entries

To list the crontab entries, we use the -l option for the current user:

```
$ crontab -l
no crontab for foo
```

The output says that there is no crontab entry for the user foo. It means the user foo has not added any task in his or her crontab yet.

To view crontab as the root user, type the following command:

```
# crontab -l
no crontab for root
```

Alternatively, use the following command:

```
$ sudo crontab -l
```

Editing crontab entries

Crontab of the current user can be edited or modified by using the -e option
with crontab:

```
$ crontab -e
```

After executing the preceding command, an editor will open where the user can
add tasks into the crontab file. In our case, the vi editor is launched. The following
entries have been added into the user foo crontab entry:

```
# My crontab entries

# On every reboot launch application firefox
@reboot firefox

# Every month run take_backup.sh script to take required backup
@monthly /home/foo/take_backup.sh

# Every day at 1:30 AM check disk space
30 1 * * * /home/foo/check-disk-space.sh
~
~
~
~
~
~
:wq
```

After saving and exiting from the editor, the output obtained is as follows:

```
no crontab for foo - using an empty one
crontab: installing new crontab
```

To view the modified crontab entry of the user foo, run the –l option again:

```
$ crontab -l
```

```
# My crontab entries

# On every reboot launch application firefox
@reboot firefox

# Every month run take_backup.sh script to take required backup
@monthly /home/foo/take_backup.sh

# Every day at 1:30 AM check disk space
30 1 * * * /home/foo/check-disk-space.sh
```

To create the `crontab` entry of the user root, we can run `crontab` with the `-e` option as the root:

```
# crontab -e
```

OR

```
$ sudo crontab -e
```

After running the preceding command, the editor opens to modify `crontab` for the user root that looks as follows after adding entries:

```
# Crontab of user root

# Start monitoring network usage by each user
@reboot /root/users_network_monitor.sh

# Take daily back at 4 AM
0 4 * * * /root/back_script.sh


~
~
~
~
:wq
```

To view the `crontab` entry of the root, we can use `crontab -l` as the root user:

```
# crontab -l
```

```
# Crontab of user root

# Start monitoring network usage by each user
@reboot /root/users_network_monitor.sh

# Take daily back at 4 AM
0 4 * * * /root/back_script.sh
```

The root user can also view and modify the `crontab` entry of another user. This is done by specifying the `-u` option followed by the username:

```
# crontab -u foo -e  # Modifying crontab of user foo as root
```

Crontab of the user foo will be opened for modification as follows:

```
# My crontab entries

# On every reboot launch application firefox
@reboot firefox

# Every month run take_backup.sh script to take required backup
@monthly /home/foo/take_backup.sh

# Every day at 1:30 AM check disk space
30 1 * * * /home/foo/check-disk-space.sh

# Run this cleanup script on every sunday
* * * * 0 /home/foo/cleanup_script.sh█
~
~
~
~
-- INSERT --
```

To view the crontab entry of another user, run the -l option with -u as follows:

```
# crontab -u foo -l
```

We can display the crontab of the user foo as follows:

```
# My crontab entries

# On every reboot launch application firefox
@reboot firefox

# Every month run take_backup.sh script to take required backup
@monthly /home/foo/take_backup.sh

# Every day at 1:30 AM check disk space
30 1 * * * /home/foo/check-disk-space.sh

# Run this cleanup script on every sunday
* * * * 0 /home/foo/cleanup script.sh
```

Crontab entries are created using the crontab command and are stored in the /var/spool/cron/ directory. A file is created by the name of the user:

```
# ls /var/spool/cron
root   foo
```

We can see that a file is created for the users root and foo.

Removing crontab entries

We can also remove `crontab` using the `-r` option with the `crontab` command. By default, `crontab` of the current user is deleted. Using the option with `-i` allows the interactive removal of crontab:

```
# crontab -i -r
crontab: really delete root's crontab? Y
```

By running the preceding command, the `crontab` entry of the user root has been deleted. We can verify this by running the `-l` option:

```
# crontab -l
no crontab for root


#  ls /var/spool/cron
foo
```

The user root can also delete `crontab` of other users by specifying the user in the `-u` option:

```
# crontab -r -i -u foo
crontab: really delete foo's crontab? n
```

We specified 'n' (no) instead of 'y' (yes), so the removal of the user `foo crontab` will be aborted.

Let's delete this now:

```
# crontab -r -i -u foo
crontab: really delete foo's crontab? Y
```

Now, the `crontab` entry of the user `foo` has been removed. To verify, run the following command:

```
$  crontab -l
no crontab for foo
```

systemd

Nowadays, most of the Linux distribution systems such as Fedora, Ubuntu, Arch Linux, Debian, openSUSE, and so on, have switched from init to systemd. systemd is the first process that gets started after system boot-up with PID 1. It controls and manages other processes that should be started after the system boot-up. It is also known as basic building block for an operating system. To learn about an init-based system, refer to the Wikipedia link at `https://en.wikipedia.org/wiki/Init`.

systemd units

systemd has several units, each containing a configuration file with information about a service, socket, device, mount point, swap file or partition, start-up target, and so on.

The following table explains some of unit files:

Unit type	File extension	Description
Service unit	`.service`	A system service
Device unit	`.device`	A device file recognized by kernel
Mount unit	`.mount`	A file system mount point
Timer unit	`.timer`	A systemd timer
Swap unit	`.swap`	A swap file

To list all the installed unit files in a system, run the `systemctl` command with the `list-unit-files` option:

```
$ systemctl list-unit-files | head -n 12
```

```
UNIT FILE                              STATE
proc-sys-fs-binfmt_misc.automount      static
dev-hugepages.mount                    static
dev-mqueue.mount                       static
proc-fs-nfsd.mount                     static
proc-sys-fs-binfmt_misc.mount          static
sys-fs-fuse-connections.mount          static
sys-kernel-config.mount                static
sys-kernel-debug.mount                 static
tmp.mount                              static
var-lib-nfs-rpc_pipefs.mount           static
cups.path                              enabled
```

To list unit files of a unit type, use the `list-unit-files` and `--type` options. Running the following command will show only a service unit available in the system:

```
$ systemctl list-unit-files --type=service | head -n 10
```

```
UNIT FILE                        STATE
abrt-ccpp.service                enabled
abrt-journal-core.service        disabled
abrt-oops.service                enabled
abrt-pstoreoops.service          disabled
abrt-vmcore.service              enabled
abrt-xorg.service                enabled
abrtd.service                    enabled
accounts-daemon.service          enabled
alsa-restore.service             static
```

Managing services

systemd manages all the available services in a system, from the time of Linux kernel boot up till the shutdown of the system. A service in a Linux system is an application that runs in the background or is waiting to be used. Service management files have the suffix `.service` in its file name.

In systemd-based Linux system, a user or an administrator can manage services using the `systemctl` command.

Status of a service

To list the current status of services and check whether it is running or not, use `systemctl status`:

For example, to see the status of my `NetworkManager` service, run the following command:

```
$ systemctl status -l NetworkManager.service
```

```
● NetworkManager.service - Network Manager
   Loaded: loaded (/usr/lib/systemd/system/NetworkManager.service; enabled
; vendor preset: enabled)
   Active: active (running) since Thu 2015-09-24 10:32:17 IST; 2 days ago
 Main PID: 779 (NetworkManager)
   CGroup: /system.slice/NetworkManager.service
           ├─  779 /usr/sbin/NetworkManager --no-daemon
           └─24346 /sbin/dhclient -d -q -sf /usr/libexec/nm-dhcp-helper -p
f /var/run/dhclient-wlp4s0.pid -lf /var/lib/NetworkManager/dhclient-26b3a3
8c-5737-4759-98f4-e6953b769fa5-wlp4s0.lease -cf /var/lib/NetworkManager/dh
client-wlp4s0.conf wlp4s0

Sep 27 00:36:05 carbon dhclient[24346]: DHCPREQUEST on wlp4s0 to 192.168.1
.1 port 67 (xid=0x9baf4314)
Sep 27 00:36:05 carbon dhclient[24346]: DHCPACK from 192.168.1.1 (xid=0x9b
af4314)
Sep 27 00:36:05 carbon NetworkManager[779]: <info>     address 192.168.1.10
6
Sep 27 00:36:05 carbon NetworkManager[779]: <info>     plen 24 (255.255.255
.0)
Sep 27 00:36:05 carbon NetworkManager[779]: <info>     gateway 192.168.1.1
Sep 27 00:36:05 carbon NetworkManager[779]: <info>     server identifier 19
2.168.1.1
Sep 27 00:36:05 carbon NetworkManager[779]: <info>     lease time 7200
Sep 27 00:36:05 carbon NetworkManager[779]: <info>     nameserver '192.168.
1.1'
Sep 27 00:36:05 carbon NetworkManager[779]: <info>     (wlp4s0): DHCPv4 state
 changed bound -> bound
Sep 27 00:36:05 carbon dhclient[24346]: bound to 192.168.1.106 -- renewal
in 2775 seconds.
```

We can see that the `NetworkManager` service is running and is in active state. It also provides detailed information associated with the current `NetworkManager` service.

Let's see status of another service called the `sshd`. The `sshd` service controls whether `ssh` connection is possible to a system or not:

```
$ systemctl status sshd.service
```

```
● sshd.service - OpenSSH server daemon
   Loaded: loaded (/usr/lib/systemd/system/sshd.service; disabled; vendor
preset: enabled)
   Active: inactive (dead)
     Docs: man:sshd(8)
           man:sshd_config(5)
```

This shows that service `sshd` is inactive currently.

If no verbose output is required, then we can just use the `is-active` option to see a service status:

```
$ systemctl is-active sshd.service
unknown
$ systemctl is-active NetworkManager.service
active
```

Here, `active` means a service is running and `unknown` means a service is not running.

Enabling and disabling services

When a system is booted, systemd automatically starts some of the services. A few of the services may not be running as well. To enable a service to run after a system is booted, use `systemctl enable` and to stop a service running by a system during boot time, use `systemctl disable`.

Executing the following command will allow systemd to run the `sshd` service after a system is booted up:

```
# systemctl enable sshd.service
```

Executing the following command will allow systemd to not run `sshd.service` when a system is booted up:

```
# systemctl disable sshd.service
```

To check whether a service is enabled or not, run the `systemctl is-enabled` command:

```
$ systemctl is-enabled sshd.service
disabled
$ systemctl is-enabled NetworkManager.service
enabled
```

It means that the `sshd` service is disabled currently during the system start-up, while the `NetworkManager` service is enabled during the start-up by `systemd`.

Start and stop a service

When a system is running, sometimes we may need some services running. For example, to do `ssh` in my current system from another system, the `sshd` service must be running.

For example, let's see what the current status of the `sshd` service is:

```
$ systemctl is-active sshd.service
unknown
```

The `sshd` service is not running currently. Let's try to do `ssh` in a system:

```
$ ssh foo@localhost  # Doing ssh to same machine  # Doing ssh to same
machine
 ssh: connect to host localhost port 22: Connection refused
```

We can see that the `ssh` connection has been refused.

Now, let's start running the `sshd` service. We can start a service by using the `systemctl start` command as follows:

```
# systemctl start sshd.service
$ systemctl is-active sshd.service
active
```

Now, the `sshd` service is running. Try doing `ssh` into the machine again:

```
$ ssh foo@localhost
Last login: Fri Sep 25 23:10:21 2015 from 192.168.1.101
```

Now, the login has been done successfully.

We can even restart a running service using the `systemctl restart` command. This is required when a service has been modified. Then, to enable the modified setting, we can just restart it.

```
#  systemctl restart sshd.service
```

The preceding command will restart the `sshd` service.

When `ssh` is no longer required, it's safe to stop running it. This avoids an anonymous access to a machine. To stop running a service, run the `systemctl stop` command:

```
# systemctl stop sshd.service
$ systemctl is-active sshd.service
unknown
```

Viewing system logs

To check whether a user is working on an individual or enterprise machine, viewing system logs is very important in order to trace a problem and get detailed information of activities happening in a system. Viewing system logs plays an important role in monitoring and ensuring network traffics are not vulnerable. On a systemd-based system, system logs are collected and managed by one of its component called journald. Its task is to collect a log of applications and kernel. Log files are available in the /var/log/journal/ directory.

To view a log collected by journald, the journalctl command is used:

```
# journalctl
```

Running the preceding command displays all system logs collected, starting from old and grows down to newer logs.

Viewing the latest log entries

To see the latest log entries and continuously printing new entries as appended to the journal, use the -f option:

```
$ journalctl -f
```

```
-- Logs begin at Thu 2015-06-11 00:59:22 IST. --
Sep 27 01:22:20 carbon dbus[673]: [system] Successfully activated service
'org.freedesktop.nm_dispatcher'
Sep 27 01:22:20 carbon systemd[1]: Started Network Manager Script Dispatch
er Service.
Sep 27 01:22:20 carbon audit[1]: <audit-1130> pid=1 uid=0 auid=4294967295
ses=4294967295 subj=system_u:system_r:init_t:s0 msg='unit=NetworkManager-d
ispatcher comm="systemd" exe="/usr/lib/systemd/systemd" hostname=? addr=?
terminal=? res=success'
Sep 27 01:22:20 carbon nm-dispatcher[3061]: Dispatching action 'dhcp4-chan
ge' for wlp4s0
Sep 27 01:22:30 carbon audit[1]: <audit-1131> pid=1 uid=0 auid=4294967295
ses=4294967295 subj=system_u:system_r:init_t:s0 msg='unit=NetworkManager-d
ispatcher comm="systemd" exe="/usr/lib/systemd/systemd" hostname=? addr=?
terminal=? res=success'
Sep 27 01:23:12 carbon avahi-daemon[687]: Invalid response packet from hos
t 192.168.1.101.
Sep 27 01:24:52 carbon avahi-daemon[687]: Invalid response packet from hos
t 192.168.1.101.
Sep 27 01:26:31 carbon avahi-daemon[687]: Invalid response packet from hos
t 192.168.1.101.
Sep 27 01:28:11 carbon avahi-daemon[687]: Invalid response packet from hos
t 192.168.1.101.
Sep 27 01:29:52 carbon avahi-daemon[687]: Invalid response packet from hos
t 192.168.1.101.
```

To see the log entries captured since the last boot of a system, use the –b option:

```
$ journalctl -b
```

```
-- Logs begin at Thu 2015-06-11 00:59:22 IST, end at Sun 2015-09-27 01:36:
Sep 24 10:32:05 carbon systemd-journal[134]: Runtime journal (/run/log/jou
                                              Maximum allowed usage is set
                                              Leaving at least 575.1M free
                                              Enforced usage limit is thus
Sep 24 10:32:05 carbon systemd-journal[134]: Runtime journal (/run/log/jou
                                              Maximum allowed usage is set
                                              Leaving at least 575.1M free
                                              Enforced usage limit is thus
Sep 24 10:32:05 carbon kernel: Initializing cgroup subsys cpuset
Sep 24 10:32:05 carbon kernel: Initializing cgroup subsys cpu
Sep 24 10:32:05 carbon kernel: Initializing cgroup subsys cpuacct
Sep 24 10:32:05 carbon kernel: Linux version 4.1.6-201.fc22.x86_64 (mockbu
Sep 24 10:32:05 carbon kernel: Command line: BOOT_IMAGE=/boot/vmlinuz-4.1.
```

Viewing logs of a particular time interval

We can also view logs of a particular time interval. For example, to view logs of the last 1 hour, we can run the following command:

```
$ journalctl --since "1 hour ago" --until now
```

To view log entries since July 1, 2015 until now, we can run the following command:

```
$ journalctl --since 2015-07-01
```

To view logs from Aug 7, 2015 at 7:23 PM to Aug 9, 2015 at 7 AM, we can run the following command:

```
$ journalctl --since "2015-08-07 19:23:00" --until "2015-08-09 7:00:00"
```

Embedding languages

Shell scripting provides a certain set of features as compared to what we get in other scripted programming languages such as Python, Ruby, Perl, and AWK. These languages provide additional features as compared to what we get in a shell script language. On Linux and UNIX-based system, to use these languages, we have to install them separately if they are not preinstalled.

Consider a simple example: there is a json or XML file and we want to parse it and retrieve the data stored in it. It's very hard and error-prone to do this using shell and its commands, but if we are aware of the Python or Ruby languages, we can easily do it and then embed it into a shell script. Embedding another language in a shell script should be done to reduce the effort and also to achieve better performance.

The syntax for embedding other languages in a shell script is as follows:

Scripting language	The syntax of embedding into a shell script
Python (Python version 2)	`python -c ''`. Inside single quotes write the Python code to be processed
Python3	`python3 -c ''`. Inside single quotes write the Python version 3 code to be processed
Perl	`perl -e ''`. Inside single quotes write the Perl code.
Ruby	`ruby -e ''`. Inside single quotes write the Ruby code.
AWK	This can be used as a command utility. Refer to the awk man page for available options.

Embedding Python language

To embed Python language inside a shell script, we will use `python -c " Python Code"`. To learn about Python, refer to the official website at `https://www.python.org/`.

A simple Python example would be printing `Hello World` in Python, which is done as follows:

```
print "Hello World"
```

To embed this in a shell script, we can write the code as follows

```
#!/bin/bash
# Filename: python_print.sh
# Description: Embeding python in shell script

# Printing using Python
python -c 'print "Hello World"'
```

We will now execute the `python_print.sh` script as follows:

```
$ sh python_print.sh
Hello World
```

To embed multiple lines of Python code in a shell script, use the following code:

```
python -  <<EOF
# Python code
EOF
```

Here, **python -** instructs the python command to take the input from stdin and EOF is a label that instructs to take the stdin input until it encounters the EOF text.

The following example embeds Python language in a shell script and fetches unread e-mails from the user's Gmail account:

```
#!/bin/bash
# Filename: mail_fetch.sh
# Description: Fetching unread email from gmail by embedding python in
shell script

# Enter username and password of your gmail account
echo Enter your gmail username:
read USER
echo Enter password:
read -s PASSWD

echo Running python code
python - <<CODE
# Importing required Python module

import urllib2
import getpass
import xml.etree.ElementTree as ET

# Function to get unread messages in XML format
def get_unread_msgs(user, passwd):
    auth_handler = urllib2.HTTPBasicAuthHandler()
    auth_handler.add_password(
        realm='mail.google.com',
        uri='https://mail.google.com',
        user=user,
        passwd=passwd
    )
    opener = urllib2.build_opener(auth_handler)
    urllib2.install_opener(opener)
```

```
        feed = urllib2.urlopen('https://mail.google.com/mail/feed/atom')
        return feed.read()

xml_data = get_unread_msgs("$USER", "$PASSWD")
root = ET.fromstring(xml_data)

# Getting Title of unread emails
print "Title of unread messages:"
print "......................"
count=0
for e in root.iter('{http://purl.org/atom/ns#}title'):
    print e.text

CODE

echo "Done!"
```

After executing this script, the sample output looks as follows:

```
$ sh mail_fetch.sh
Enter your gmail username:
foo@gmail.com
Enter password:

Running python code
Title of unread messages:
.....................................
Gmail - Inbox for foo@gmail.com
Unread message1
unread message2
Unread message3
Done!
```

Embedding AWK language

Awk is a programming language designed for text processing and is mainly used for fetching relevant data and for reporting tools. To learn more about AWK programming language, refer to its man page or visit the website at http://www.gnu.org/software/gawk/manual/gawk.html.

The Awk language can be very easily used in a shell script. For example, consider the output of the `df` command on a running system:

```
$ df -h
```

```
Filesystem      Size  Used Avail Use% Mounted on
devtmpfs        3.8G     0  3.8G   0% /dev
tmpfs           3.8G  128K  3.8G   1% /dev/shm
tmpfs           3.8G  1.2M  3.8G   1% /run
tmpfs           3.8G     0  3.8G   0% /sys/fs/cgroup
/dev/sda1        38G   21G   15G  59% /
tmpfs           3.8G  9.3M  3.8G   1% /tmp
/dev/dm-0       197G   99G   88G  53% /home
tmpfs           767M     0  767M   0% /run/user/990
tmpfs           767M   40K  767M   1% /run/user/1000
```

To fetch the fourth column — that is, the `Avail` field using `awk` — we can write a shell script using `awk` as follows:

```
#!/bin/bash
# Filename: awk_embed.sh
# Description: Demonstrating using awk in shell script

# Fetching 4th column of command df output
df -h |awk '{ print $4 }'
```

```
Avail
3.8G
3.8G
3.8G
3.8G
15G
3.8G
88G
767M
767M
```

Consider another example in which we will use an input file that will be the `/etc/passwd` file of a system. This file contains the basic information about each user or account on a Linux or UNIX-based system.

Each line of a `/etc/passwd` file looks as follows:

root:x:0:0:root:/root:/bin/bash

There are seven fields and each field is separated by a colon (:). To learn the detailed meaning of each field, refer to the Wikipedia link at `https://en.wikipedia.org/wiki/Passwd`.

The following shell script makes use of awk features and displays some useful information from the /etc/passwd file. For example, we will consider the following as the content of the passwd file:

```
$ cat passwd
root:x:0:0:root:/root:/bin/bash
bin:x:1:1:bin:/bin:/sbin/nologin
daemon:x:2:2:daemon:/sbin:/sbin/nologin
adm:x:3:4:adm:/var/adm:/sbin/nologin
lp:x:4:7:lp:/var/spool/lpd:/sbin/nologin
sync:x:5:0:sync:/sbin:/bin/sync
shutdown:x:6:0:shutdown:/sbin:/sbin/shutdown
halt:x:7:0:halt:/sbin:/sbin/halt


$ cat passwd_file_info.sh      # Shell script content
#!/bin/bash
# Filename: passwd_file_info.sh
# Desciption: Fetches useful information from /etc/passwd file using awk


# Fetching 1st and 3rd field i.e. Username and UID and separate them with
blank space
awk -F":" '{ print "Username: " $1 "\tUID:" $3 }' passwd


# Searching line whose user is root
echo "User root information"
awk '$1 ~ /^root/' passwd
```

Running this script gives following result:

```
$ sh passwd_file_info.sh
Username: root   UID:0
Username: bin    UID:1
Username: daemon         UID:2
Username: adm    UID:3
Username: lp     UID:4
Username: sync   UID:5
```

```
Username: shutdown        UID:6
Username: halt  UID:7


User root information
root:x:0:0:root:/root:/bin/bash
```

 It is also possible to use compiled languages such as C, C++, and Java in a shell script. To do so, write commands to compile and execute the code.

Summary

After reading this chapter, you should now know how to schedule a task to be performed at a specific time using the at command. You should also know the benefits of creating Cron jobs, which need to be performed multiple times. You should have also learned how to use the crontab command to add, modify, list, and remove crontab entries. You also have a good understanding of systemd—the first process created on a system—and how it manages other system processes, services, and logs. You should also know how to embed other scripting languages such as Python, AWK, Ruby, and so on, in a shell script.

After reading all of these chapters and practicing the examples, you should now be confident in shell scripting. Being a master of the command line, you are now capable of writing your own shell scripts to solve your day-to-day tasks. Finally, if anything is not covered in this book, you know that you should look into the man page of any command for help.

Index

Exit code 128+n 76
with special meaning 75, 76
expressions, testing with test command
about 79
arithmetic checks 81, 82
expression checks 83, 84
file checks 79-81
string checks 82, 83

F

files
comparing 171
comparing, diff command used 172, 173
configuration files 190
content, viewing with cat command 165
copying 168, 169
copying locally 169
copying remotely, scp command used 170
copying, to another location 170
copying, to remote server 171
creating 162
deleting 166
directory, deleting 167
directory file 162
directory, moving to new location 169
finding and deleting, based on inode
number 176
link, creating 176
moving 168
opened files list, obtaining 188
ownership 183
permissions 183
regular file 162
regular file, deleting 167
renaming 169
searching 174, 175
searching, according to use case 175, 176
special files 178
temporary files 182
viewing 165
viewing, less command used 166
viewing, ls command used 165
viewing, more command used 166
for loop
about 93
command output, iterating over 94

range, specifying 95
simple iteration 93, 94
format modifiers
defining 4
format specification
used, for printing different data
type format 4
functions
calling in bash 104
parameters, passing to 105
using 103, 104

G

grep command
exact word, matching 47
filename, displaying with matching
pattern 47
files/directories, excluding from
search 46, 47
multiple substitutions 50
output, editing with sed command 48, 49
searching, in a binary file 45, 46
searching, in a directory 46
syntax 41-43
used, for filtering output 40
uses 45
grep command, options
-a 41
-A NUM 41
-B NUM 41
-c 41
-C NUM 41
-E 41
-e PATTERN 41
-f FILE 41
-i 41
-n 41
-o 41
-q 41
-r 41
-R 41
-v 41
s 41
pattern, searching in multiple files 43-45

Thank you for buying
Linux Shell Scripting Essentials

About Packt Publishing

Packt, pronounced 'packed', published its first book, *Mastering phpMyAdmin for Effective MySQL Management*, in April 2004, and subsequently continued to specialize in publishing highly focused books on specific technologies and solutions.

Our books and publications share the experiences of your fellow IT professionals in adapting and customizing today's systems, applications, and frameworks. Our solution-based books give you the knowledge and power to customize the software and technologies you're using to get the job done. Packt books are more specific and less general than the IT books you have seen in the past. Our unique business model allows us to bring you more focused information, giving you more of what you need to know, and less of what you don't.

Packt is a modern yet unique publishing company that focuses on producing quality, cutting-edge books for communities of developers, administrators, and newbies alike. For more information, please visit our website at www.packtpub.com.

About Packt Open Source

In 2010, Packt launched two new brands, Packt Open Source and Packt Enterprise, in order to continue its focus on specialization. This book is part of the Packt Open Source brand, home to books published on software built around open source licenses, and offering information to anybody from advanced developers to budding web designers. The Open Source brand also runs Packt's Open Source Royalty Scheme, by which Packt gives a royalty to each open source project about whose software a book is sold.

Writing for Packt

We welcome all inquiries from people who are interested in authoring. Book proposals should be sent to author@packtpub.com. If your book idea is still at an early stage and you would like to discuss it first before writing a formal book proposal, then please contact us; one of our commissioning editors will get in touch with you.

We're not just looking for published authors; if you have strong technical skills but no writing experience, our experienced editors can help you develop a writing career, or simply get some additional reward for your expertise.

Linux Mint Essentials

ISBN: 978-1-78216-815-7   Paperback: 324 pages

A practical guide to Linux Mint for the novice to the professional

1. Learn to use Linux Mint like a pro, starting with the installation and going all the way through maintaining your system.

2. Covers everything you need to know in order to be productive, including browsing the Internet, creating documents, and installing software.

3. Hands-on activities reinforce your knowledge.

Linux Mint System Administration Beginner's Guide

ISBN: 978-1-84951-960-1   Paperback: 146 pages

A practical guide to learn basic concepts, techniques, and tools to become a Linux Mint system administrator

1. Discover Linux Mint and learn how to install it.

2. Learn basic shell commands and how to deal with user accounts.

3. Find out how to carry out system administrator tasks such as monitoring, backups, and network configuration.

Please check www.PacktPub.com for information on our titles

www.ingramcontent.com/pod-product-compliance
Lightning Source LLC
Chambersburg PA
CBHW060526060326
40690CB00017B/3399